Indian Gold Jewellery Industry

India has a long-standing cultural and societal affinity with gold and gold jewellery. Gold metaphorically represents the sacredness, purity and immortality that bind religious beliefs and culture together. Accumulation of gold is associated with material and non-material cultures where the perceptions, attitudes and experiences of the members engaged in production and consumption are bound into a complex relationship. The idea of the book initially originated from the course of research work. It was found that India has the largest unorganised jewellery industry, in terms of manufacturing and consumption unit. Jewellery fabrication in India is not just a profession for the jewellers, but it has been a family tradition extending across generations. Gold jewellery makers (*sunnar, swarnakars*) are the spine of the jewellery industry. They acquired the skill of making jewellery from the experienced and learned gold smithery (*karigars*), either from their ancestors who were engaged in this business or from the craftsmen-cum-petty traders. The co-relations of castes, religion, culture, economy and class were intertwined with each other in such a way that made the gold jewellery industry sustainable. Surprisingly, there is an absence of literature on understanding the structural and functional aspects of the gold jewellery industry in India.

This book explores the roles of *sunars/swarnakars* (goldsmith or jewellery makers), consumers, trade and the policies that bring a change in the gold jewellery industry in India and India's position in the global market scenario. By focusing on their way of life, the book brings unique insights into the social and economic experience of the unorganised gold jewellery sector and the role of consumers in production.

Sylvia Raha, Assistant Professor at the School of Social Sciences, Ramaiah University of Applied Sciences, and former faculty at North Bengal St Xavier's College. With over a decade of academic expertise, she has extensively taught sociology and public policy. Her PhD research delves into economic sociology, exploring themes such as market, media, work, occupation, consumption and consumer culture, alongside cultural studies. Her current research focus revolves around health studies and AI, offering a unique perspective rooted in economic sociology principles.

Routledge Focus on Management and Society

Series Editor: Anindya Sen
Pro Vice-Chancellor, School of Social Sciences,
Ramaiah University of Applied Sciences, India

The aim of the Focus series is to present the reader with a number of short volumes which deal with important managerial issues in the Indian context. Volumes already published in the series cover topics which are of perennial interest to managers, like strategic change and transformation, and supply chain management, as well as emerging areas of research like neuro-marketing and digital culture. CEOs today also need to be familiar with critical developments in other fields, like auction theory and the contribution of sociology to management thinking. A forthcoming volume examines the law of one price in the context of dually listed shares, i.e., shares which are listed in both Indian stock markets and abroad. In other words, the Focus series is designed to introduce management theorists and researchers (as well as the general public) to a diverse set of topics relevant directly or peripherally to management in a short, readable format, without sacrificing basic rigour and set in the Indian context.

Excellence in Supply Chain Management
Balram Avittathur and Debabrata Ghosh

Digital Cultures
Smeeta Mishra

Artificial Intelligence, Business and Civilization
Our Fate Made in Machines
Andreas Kaplan

Law of One Price
A Chronicle of Dually Listed Indian Stocks
Vinodh Madhavan and Partha Ray

For more information about this series, please visit: www.routledge.com/ Routledge-Focus-on-Management-and-Society/book-series/RFMS

Indian Gold Jewellery Industry
Culture and Consumption

Sylvia Raha

Routledge
Taylor & Francis Group

LONDON AND NEW YORK

First published 2024
by Routledge
2 Park Square, Milton Park, Abingdon, Oxon OX14 4RN

and by Routledge
605 Third Avenue, New York, NY 10158

Routledge is an imprint of the Taylor & Francis Group, an information business

British Library Cataloguing-in-Publication Data
A catalogue record for this book is available from the British Library

ISBN: 978-1-032-71793-7 (hbk)
ISBN: 978-1-032-71794-4 (pbk)
ISBN: 978-1-032-71795-1 (ebk)

DOI: 10.4324/9781032717951

Typeset in Times New Roman
by MPS Limited, Dehradun

To my precious miracle, Udvaahni:
Your arrival has brought light to my life. This book is
dedicated to the boundless love and hope you've brought
into our lives.

Contents

Figures and Charts

Tables

Preface

My inclination towards identifying and knowing the hereditary Indian jewellers, popularly known as *swarnakars* or *sonars,* was cultivated when all the jewellers in India went for a national strike in the year 2012. This book is the culmination of my desire to uncover the tales behind the craftsmanship, trade, legacy of precious ornaments and the market. Additionally, it delves into the cultural ethos that maintains and sustains the artistry of making gold jewellery. It was my PhD research area, where my search was driven by a deep curiosity, aiming to unravel not only the everyday life of the jewellers, *karigars* and their craftsmanship but also the intricate economic-sociological aspects woven into the industry. Beyond the gleam of gold, jewellery encapsulates cultural identity and socio-cultural uniqueness that intertwines with religious practices to influence the economic dimensions of producers, manufacturers and consumers across generations.

Over the course of my academic journey, I realised that a comprehensive exploration is required to bridge the gap in our understanding of how these artisans adapt and evolve to changing times. I started with investigating historical narratives that have shaped social connections. From these investigations, I found that it is not just about mastering new techniques for crafting jewellery or adopting modern marketing strategies – it is a sequence of events of survival and change. The *swarnakars,* who have passed down their art through generations, suddenly find themselves at a crossroads due to changes in governmental policies and the coming up of corporate jewellery sectors. For them, it is more than just a job; it is their identity and status intertwined into the fabric of their social existence.

I hope this book aspires to provide a comprehensive overview of Indian jewellers and their lives, offering readers a glimpse into a world of creativity, dedication and tradition.

Dr Sylvia Raha

Acknowledgement

My journey into the intricate world of the 'gold jewellery industry' commenced during my PhD research at the University of North Bengal. My heartfelt gratitude goes to Prof. Sanjay Kumar Roy, my PhD supervisor, for his unwavering support that empowered me to wholeheartedly delve into this topic for research.

The fruition of this book stands as a testament to the extraordinary guidance extended by Prof. Anindya Sen, formerly Professor of Economics, Indian Institute of Management Calcutta. His support and mentorship transformed a section of my PhD research into the form of a comprehensive book that I present today. Prof. Anindya Sen's profound influence has refined my research on the Indian jewellery industry. His indelible imprint is woven into every page of this book, standing as a testament to the profound impact of his mentorship, which has elevated this project to its current stature.

I sincerely thank Dr Satyam Sil, Consultant Epidemiologist at NCDC, Delhi, whose thorough examination of my manuscript and insightful commentary contributed significantly to its depth and relevance. Dr Sanchita Sil's constructive feedback on the book is deeply appreciated.

I am profoundly thankful to my mother Soma Raha and my father Debabrata Raha for providing me with a nurturing environment and unwavering mental support throughout the process of writing the manuscript.

Last, my appreciation extends to the publisher for recognising the value of my manuscript and facilitating its journey to reach its intended readership.

Dr Sylvia Raha

1   The Global Scenario of Gold Consumption

Gold: Both a Commodity and Money

Gold has been one of the most desirable commodities that is commercially used throughout history. It is the only precious metal which is connected with money, wealth, culture, emotions (sometimes irrational), jewellery, investment, technology and central bank demand. Gold as a commodity can control other commodities in exchange for money – what Karl Marx referred to as a commodity's 'value'. When it satisfies certain human needs, it is called 'use-value' by Adam Smith. The value of gold as a commodity is constant in terms of quality but the only differences lie in the quantity of value of gold (Bottomore, 2000, p. 101). Before 1914, the Bank of England and its associated countries managed the gold standard solely working with it as a central banking system. The countries on the gold standard[1] were: Sweden, France, Finland, Netherlands, Norway, Denmark, Belgium, Russia, German, Japan, Italy and Austria-Hungary. Starting in the 1870s, these countries adopted the gold standard system to promote international trade and stability by providing a common standard for the value of money. Due to the ability of these countries to settle their obligations with one another in gold, gold functioned as a medium of exchange in international trade as well. This made trading easier by giving people a reliable, acknowledged method of payment that could be used everywhere. Until 1914, all the countries fixed the value of their currencies in terms of the quantity/weight and quality/purity of gold for trading and investment purposes.

After 1914, the start of World War I significantly influenced the status of the international gold standard. Most of the world's major economies were on the gold standard, which meant that they tied the value of their respective currencies to a certain amount of gold. So, when the conflict began, the ability to convert national currencies into gold was suspended. This caused several countries to be forced to print money to pay for their war efforts, which led to currency devaluation and inflation.

DOI: 10.4324/9781032717951-1

As a result, both the gold standard and the global monetary system were impacted.

Attempts were made to reinstate the gold standard after the war, but it was ineffective because of the complex economic and political situations in many major countries. Some countries, such as Germany and Austria-Hungary, could not meet their obligations under the gold standard and eventually abandoned it. However, France and the United States kept their currencies pegged to gold but had only a restricted ability to convert their currencies into gold. The system was further weakened by competitive devaluations, trade restrictions and the reduction in the supply of gold because of the closure of gold mines during World War I and the 1930s Great Depression (Bloomfield, 1959, 1981). The gold market transformed from a monetary function to a distributional one, ultimately causing the failure of the gold standard. As a result, the international community formalised a new monetary system, the Bretton Woods system, during the 1944 Bretton Woods conference after World War II, in order to functionalise this monetary exchange.

At this conference, the central banks abstained from adapting to a new free market for gold as it was getting harder to determine the precise weight and purity of gold for international monetary exchange; but agreed to measure the value of gold without domestic convertibility in terms of a fixed-exchange rate of US dollar values ($35 per ounce of gold). So, they created a fixed-exchange rate to stabilise unfettered investment and trade. Being the wealthiest country, the United States became the sole official country for reserve currency in terms of the gold dollar. This agreement continued through the 1960s. However, in 1971 this system collapsed when President Nixon decided to stop allowing other countries to convert US dollars into gold, as major trading countries were unable to maintain the value of their currencies to the gold dollar's value. It ultimately forced the United States to quit its position as a global leader in 1971 because of a decline in the gold reserves. Convertibility of gold into dollars became a major issue for the major trading countries and other 'countries built up a balance with dollar rather than converting it into gold'.[2] The international gold exchange standard and the fixed monetary system ended in 1973 because none of the other countries were prepared to take over the role of implementing the agreements. This shows that it is not possible to compare one gold product to another because the use-value of gold as a commodity differs qualitatively, as each gold product possesses its own unique characteristics that set it apart.

The primary factor is that gold will only be mined and produced into a marketable commodity if it can be promoted on a competitive market at a higher price that surpasses production costs along with a sufficient rate of return. For example, in 1975, the United States listed gold on its list of commodities for future trading on the major markets in New York and Chicago. Despite this development, the International Monetary Fund (IMF) remains as one of the oldest and leading official gold holders in the world. IMF continues to view gold as a significant reserve asset for both its monetary and commodity value for maintaining the stability of international market. For example, during 2008, when there was a global financial crisis run-up, IMF did not have enough money to support the countries. In order to overcome the crisis, the IMF converted the gold in its reserve stock into money and facilitated the purchase of gold by other nations, including India, to stabilise their economy.[3] Therefore, the larger producers, gold holders and big monetary authorities are controlling the current gold market.

Consumption of Gold and Gold Jewellery

Consumption is the process by which members of society use products and services. It includes the social and cultural connotations associated with the products, besides the act of purchasing and using them. From a sociological perspective, consumption is a social process that is influenced by several variables, such as economic (income, wealth and employment), socio-cultural (values, beliefs and social norms) and psychological (needs, wants and desires) aspects. Consumption and social inequality are related because it facilitates in creating and maintaining social identities. Consumers' tastes and preferences for gold jewellery are not simply a matter of personal choice, rather they are shaped by their social and economic position in society (Bourdieu, 1999 (1989)). In this contemporary society, consumerism and consumer culture have become the dominant aspect of the market structure of every country. This phase involves a constant push for people to change and update their identities, creating a sense of uncertainty and instability in their personal lives, but ultimately driving up the demand and supply of the product (Bauman, 2007).

Demand

The term, 'demand for gold consumption' can describe both as the general global market demand for gold and a specific demand for gold for specific countries (geographical areas). Global economic growth, inflation, geopolitical unrest, the price of gold and consumer demand for investments can influence the demand for gold consumption.

The global growth in demand for gold jewellery fabrication is driven by both consumer and governmental interests. With respect to 'demand' for gold consumption, the World Gold Council (WGC) reports that India and China are the top consumers of gold jewellery. The demand trend for gold fluctuates from year to year since it is controlled by investors' demand, exchange-traded funds (ETFs), demand from central banks and other factors. The global consumption of gold in terms of gold demand, jewellery fabrication,[4] technology and investment along with total counts of bars and coins, ETFs and central bank and other institutions, was evaluated by the WGC. The *Metal Focus* of WGC has highlighted data which illustrates the general trend of gold consumption in 2022. When compared with 2021 the data reveals that the total gold demand increased by 18 percent, in which gold jewellery fabrication demand has decreased by 2 percent, gold used for technology demand has decreased by 7 percent, while gold used for investment purpose has increased by 10 percent and possession of gold by Central bank and other institutions has increased by 152 percent. However, there is an increase of 2 percent only in terms of total bars and coins. This is attributed to the lockdowns following the COVID-19 pandemic across the globe in the year 2020 to a varied extent. Thus, only the last two years were considered for analysing the gold demand. In 2021, the COVID-19 pandemic continued to impact gold demand in India. The demand for gold jewellery was weak in the first half of the year as many physical jewellery stores were closed or operating at reduced capacity. Later on, the demand for gold jewellery gradually increased in the second half of 2021 as restrictions loosened. On the other side, investors saw gold investment as safe-haven assets which led to a sharp increase in demand for gold investment in 2021. Looking ahead to 2022, when the Indian economy recovered from the pandemic, it was expected that the use of gold for jewellery would increase when compared to previous years; however, one observed a fall in jewellery, technology, demand from central banks and other institutions. It was caused because of the extreme changes in the gold price. A drastic increase in the gold price and re-settling down to normal life after the pandemic led to a decline in the demand for gold jewellery (Table 1.1).

Table 1.1 Total Gold Demand in Tonnes

Year	2021	2022	Win/Loss Chart 2021 2022
Jewellery	2,230.6	2,189.8	
Technology	330.2	308.5	
Investment	1,001.9	1,106.8	
Central banks and other institutions	450.1	1,135.7	
Total Gold Demand	**4,012.8**	**4,740.7**	

Source: Metal Focus, World Gold Council 2023.
Note: Win = Highest Point (Grey), Loss = Lowest Point (Black).

The demand for gold jewellery declined to 1324 tonnes in 2020, with an ounce of gold costing an average of US$ 1769.6 as the market remained locked down because of the disruption caused by Covid-19. The global downturn in Q2 (second quarter) of 2020 saw a sharp decline of 74 percent in India, 60 percent in the Middle East, 42 percent in Europe, 34 percent in the United States.[5] But the global demand for gold jewellery increased to 2230.6 tonnes in 2021 as a result of easing of the covid-related restrictions, which increased consumer and governmental demand for manufacturing of gold jewellery. This is how market flexibility can influence both the government and consumer's interests in increasing gold demand.

Currently, comparing 2022 to the previous three years, there is an increase in the demand for gold jewellery worldwide (2019, 2020, 2021) (Table 1.2). An important factor boosting the growth of this gold jewellery demand is the increase in disposable income. Countries like India, China, Turkey and Ghana have a strong socio-cultural significance of gold jewellery, which is significantly tied with investment in gold. Gold jewellery has become very popular in India and China as a result of the expanding middle class and rising wealth, where demand is influenced by socio-cultural and economic indicators. The total consumption of gold jewellery globally has decreased by 2 percent in 2021 from 2230 tonnes to 2189.8 tonnes in 2022. Further, it is interesting to note that the demand for gold jewellery in India was higher than China by 5 percent in the year 2022.

The United States, UAE and Saudi Arabia are additional countries with considerable demand for gold jewellery. Gold jewellery is traditionally worn by the Middle East consumers as a sign of wealth, prestige and also for investment purpose. The United States gold jewellery makers have a significant market depending on economic and cultural variables that influences gold demand. In addition to the five nations, France,

Table 1.2 Top Five Countries for Jewellery Demand Trend

Countries	2020	2021	2022	3 Years Trend
India	315.9	610.9	600.4	
China, P.R.: Mainland	413.8	673.3	570.9	
United States	118.2	149.1	143.7	
UAE	21.5	33.8	46.9	
Saudi Arabia	22.7	33.3	37.9	

Source: World Gold Council, 2023.

Table 1.3 Top Five Countries for Consumer Demand for Gold

Countries	2020	2021	2022	3 Years Trend
China, P.R.: Mainland	612.7	958.8	789.2	
India	446.4	797.3	774.0	
United States	187.3	264.9	256.6	
Germany	166.0	173.7	196.4	
Turkey	147.0	95.3	121.5	

Source: World Gold Council, 2023.

Germany and Italy are the three biggest purchasers of gold jewellery in Europe.

According to the WGC, the Indian demand for gold *jewellery consumption*[6] reached 380.7 tonnes (Q1 94.2t, Q2 140.3t and Q3 146.2t) between January and September 2022 despite a slowdown in global gold demand and gold price. During the month of November 2022, the rise in gold price has affected the wedding seasons and occasional purchase. To circumvent this, the local jewellery market increased the discount on jewellery from US$14/oz (₹1,158.37) to US $30-35/oz (₹2454.652–₹2894.76) at the end of November as a result of weak demand. Table 1.3 shows that a strong consumer demand in India causes the increase in jewellery demand year-over year, although when compared to the previous year 2021, a decline in jewellery demand of 1.7 percent was observed in the year 2022, which is significantly less than China and the United States (see Table 1.2). UAE and Saudi Arabia, on the contrary, rose to the top five countries in terms of jewellery demand countries in the world. When compared to 2020 and 2021, a rise in the demand for jewellery in the UAE and Saudi Arabia was witnessed, where the demand for gold climbed by 12.13 and 13.14 percentage points, respectively, in 2022.

The WGC expects that the Indian government will maintain its support for the gold industry through initiatives like the Gold Monetization Scheme, which aims to monetise pure gold held by individuals and institutions and the Sovereign Gold Bond Scheme that allows the investors to purchase gold as paper. However, the demand for gold can be impacted by several outside variables, including shifts in governmental policies, the state of the economy and world events. We have observed that it has impacted the demand for gold in India and other countries in the past and gold demand may continue to be impacted in the future by economic uncertainties, changes in governmental policy and regulations and the COVID-19 pandemic. The second crucial element was demand for gold jewellery that had shrunk during this phase due to travel restrictions and Indian exporters were reluctant to transport gold on credit which led to a significant decline in the export of gold jewellery to the UAE.[7] The disturbances brought on by Covid-19 in 2019–20 has interrupted the flow of demand-supply of gold export, which further declined in 2020–21. The decline was severe in Q1' 2020–2021, although export growth of gold has increased in November 2020 as a result of a recovery in demand for gemstones. In 2021, India consumed 754.1 tonnes of gold according to Reserve Bank of India (RBI), implying a consumption (consumers' demand) per capita of 0.6 grams. As per Mukesh Kumar, Senior Analyst, Indian WGC RBI has increased its total holdings to 78.4 tonnes by adding 1.1 tonnes to India's gold reserve in December 2022. So, in the year 2022, RBI increased its gold holdings by 33.3 tonnes, which is 76 percent less year-over-year.[8]

The Indian gold market has a strong link with cultural and religious traditions. Gold and gold jewellery is an important component for 1.4 billion Indians as it serves both as an investment and a means for personal adornment. The market share for plain gold jewellery is still between 80 and 85 percent. Other than bridal jewellery, lightweight, studded jewellery has become increasingly popular. Bridal jewellery (50 and 55 percent of the market share) composed of 22 karat gold has long been a favourite among both manufacturers and consumers, along with an expansion of 18th karat gold jewellery. India is the second-largest consumer of jewellery in the world today.

Side by side, millennials no longer rely solely on purchasing traditional jewellery. Therefore, change in jewellery design is the new demand from the modern young people. Suvankar Sen, MD, Senco Gold and Diamonds Pvt Ltd, India also points out that 'consumer behavior has also been affected by the trend in rupee gold prices, which have touched record levels. Consumers normally have a fixed budget when they visit stores and so the amount of gold they can buy will vary with changing gold prices. As a result, over the last five to six years retailers and manufacturers have increasingly focused on lightweight products to satisfy a range of budgets. This is important, even for traditionally heavy bridal pieces and temple jewellery. As a result, I believe, over the years there has been at least a 10% drop in average product weights'.[9] The demand for lightweight jewellery has become a new trend for gold jewellery consumption in India.

E-commerce options are expanding in India in an effort to engage millennials in the gold purchase process. It has evolved to facilitate gold jewellery sales online for both casual wear and bridal wear (see Chapter 4). This platform is used by jewellery manufacturers and retailers to sell gold jewellery both domestically and overseas. In terms of regional consumption, Tamil Nadu, Andhra Pradesh and Kerala in India's south, together with Gujarat and Maharashtra in the west and West Bengal in the east, are the states that buy the most gold.

Supply

The term 'supply' refers to the quantity of gold in jewellery consumption that a manufacturer is prepared and ready to provide for sale at a specific price. Cost of production, availability of gold reserves and the demand for gold on a worldwide scale all impact the gold supply. Even the market price of gold is determined by the interaction of the supply and demand for the metal. For instance, rising demand will cause higher prices, as well as potential increases in mine output and gold recycling. The global supply of gold comes from a variety of sources including mining, recycling and central bank sales. Mining is the primary source of gold supply. Most gold mining occurs in China (332.0t), the Russian Federation (330.9t), Australia (315.1t), Canada (192 9t), the United States (186.8t) and Ghana (129.2t). Other significant gold-producing countries include Peru, Mexico, Indonesia and South Africa. China was the world's largest producer in 2021, accounting for approximately 9 percent of global output. Recycling is another significant source of gold supply. India is the fourth-largest recycler of gold, after China, Italy and the United States, according to the WGC.[10] It contributes 11 percent of the local annual supply of gold scrap. This has happened because the younger fashion-conscious consumers in India wear gold jewellery for a limited period and re-sell it for trendy jewellery. The jewellery manufacturer and retailers sell the recycled jewellery to the refineries. The Indian Good Delivery Standard (2020) was established to enable refineries in creating a chain of custody and producing bars that satisfy the gold standard which would be used for exchange. Gold is a highly recyclable metal, and any gold ever mined is still in circulation. Central bank sales, while a small percentage of the total supply, can also have an impact on the gold market. Central banks around the world hold large reserves of gold, and they can choose to sell or lease some of these reserves to other countries or to the market.

The supply of gold and gold jewellery products and services is shaped by the connections among manufacturer, producers and consumers (see Chapter 3); the producers and suppliers are more likely to influence the jewellery market by controlling the supply (export) of gold and gold jewellery. Globalisation has significantly impacted this, as multinational jewellery companies have increased their market share and power. More diverse jewellery products and services are now offered on a wide-scale, but this has also raised worries about cultural uniformity (Table 1.4).

Table 1.4 Indian Supply of Gold in Tonnes

Year	2018	2019	2020	2021	Year-on-Year Percent Change
Gross Bullion imports	871.7	827.4	399.6	1,003.4	**151**
of which dore[1]	275.9	211.5	107.6	219.6	**104**
Net bullion imports	755.7	646.8	349.5	924.6	**165**
Scrap	87.0	119.5	95.5	75.2	**−21**
Domestic supply from other sources[2]	10.5	11.1	9.0	6.9	**−23**
Total supply[3]	853.1	777.4	454.0	1,006.7	**122**

Source: World Gold Council, 2022.

Notes
[1] Amount of fine gold in the dore.
[2] Domestic supply from local mines production, recovery from imported copper concentrates and disinvestment.
[3] Three sectors are jewellery, investment and technology. The total supply figure in the table will not add to jewellery plus investment demand for India.

The largest export market for Indian gold jewellery is now the United States, which has replaced the UAE, but according to the WGC report, India still ranks among the top providers of gold jewellery globally. This reflects two changes: First, additional tariffs on Chinese jewellery exports to the Unite States have boosted Indian suppliers (exporters') competitiveness. Second, the UAE introduced a 5 percent import duty in January 2017 and a 5 percent Value Added Tax (VAT) in January 2018, both of which had a negative effect on gold suppliers' competitiveness.[11] As a result, the data presented in Table 1.4 indicates that India's total gold supply in tonnes has experienced a 122% increase from the previous year. However, it was announced in May 2022 that 90 percent of Indian gold is authorised to be supplied to UAE duty-free under the Comprehensive Economic Partnership Agreement (CEPA). This will have a wide-ranging benefit for India because gold products can be re-supplied again to other countries.

When comparing the Q3'22 and Q4'22 Indian gold supply, gross bullion imports, including dore and net bullion imports, showed a negative change in the supply of gold. However, there was an increase in scrap gold and domestic supply from local mine production and recovery from imported copper concentrates, as well as disinvestment. The supply increased from 16 tonnes in Q3'22 to 30.5 tonnes in Q4'22, showing a 53 percent year-on-year increase. This finding shows that the recycling of old gold jewellery on the domestic front has improved India's gold refining efficiency and has minimised the country's need for overseas gold leasing. It has happened as a result of a new policy known as the Revamped Gold Monetization Scheme (R-GMS) that was introduced in 2021. It has permitted and encouraged local banks to purchase locally made gold bars from Indian

Refined Gold (IGDS). Although, the yearly Indian supply growth of 2022 (782.7 tonnes) has fallen from the year 2021 (1006.7 tonnes). According to Vikas Singh, Managing Director and CEO, MMTC-PAMP India Pvt Ltd, 'as the jewellery industry has become more organised we have seen small jewellers increasingly opt to recycle gold with organized refineries. The implementation of strict pollution control norms in some cities has also negatively impacted smaller refineries and helped push business to the organized players'.[12]

The global gold market has become a full-fledged market. Gold is a valuable metal that is frequently used in jewellery, investments and industrial uses. The demand for gold fluctuates across the world depending on many variables, including monetary conditions, geo-political developments and cultural norms. In terms of jewellery consumption, China and India are two nations that consume the most gold worldwide. China is the biggest user of gold for industrial and investment uses, whereas India is the biggest consumer of gold for jewellery. Other Asian nations with a similar cultural connection to gold are seeing a rise in their desire for the metal (Menon, 2015, p. 64).

Gold Price

Gold has been used as a unit of account and a means for commerce by humans for countless years. The global gold market decodes the price of gold on a global scale depending on primary indicators that impact the price of gold over time in relation to demand and supply, political and economic developments and currency devaluations. These indicators depend on the value of the US dollar, which is usually correlated with the price of gold as it is the primary reserve currency in the world and regularly used as a benchmark in global trade and finance. Because of this, they built an inverse relationship between gold price and the US dollar, despite regional variations in gold price where the price of gold declines when the value of the US dollar rises and vice-verse.[13] The price of gold increases when demand is strong and decreases when demand is low. In short, it is important to note that the gold price is a function of various factors: including, a) When global economic conditions are unstable, investors always seek a safe space (buying/investing on gold) for their money which increases the price of gold; b) Uncertainty in global geopolitical aspects may lead to a rise in demand for gold as a haven which may directly impact the gold price, c) Other variations in supply and demand may have an impact on the gold price, d) Changes in the gold holding can affect the gold price as it depends on country-specific factors and e) The price of gold is affected by the costs of mining the metal. Higher mining expenses may cause higher pricing of gold, whilst lower mining price may cause competitive price.

Table 1.5 Average-Annual Gold Price as per ICE Benchmark Administration

Last 5 Years Currency symbol	US Dollar US$/oz	Indian Rupees Rs/10 g
2018	1,268.5	2,7861.26384
2019	1,392.6	3,1542.48975
2020	1,769.6	4,2181.7337
2021	1,798.6	4,2750.13265
2022	1,800.1	4,5437.48578

Source: ICE Benchmark Administration,[15] World Gold Council.

The average gold price can fluctuate significantly from year to year. In the past five years, there has been a significant rise in the price of gold across the globe. Table 1.5 lists the average-annual Gold Price as per ICE Benchmark Administration[14] from 2018 to 2022.

The analysis reveals a consistent upward trend in global gold prices from 2018 to 2022. In 2018, the price of gold was recorded at Rs 2,7861.2 per 10 grams. The price of gold saw considerable volatility throughout this year because of a variety of causes. The US-China trade conflict, the Brexit discussions and other global geopolitical issues have put pressure on the gold market, which increased demand for gold as a safe-haven asset. By 2019, the price of gold had increased to Rs 3,1542.4, showing a rise of approximately 13 percent because the US Federal Reserve reduced the interest rate thus boosting the demand for gold, the hostilities between the United States and Iran increased tensions in the Middle East that led to a rise in a gold price; and as a result of all these, gold price increased by 9.8 percent in US dollars for miners. A similar trend was observed in large producing nations like Australia and Canada, as well as for purchasers of large consumption countries like India, Germany and Turkey.

The year 2020 saw a significant increase in the price of gold, reaching Rs 4,2181.7, a rise of approximately 33 percent from 2019. This increase can be attributed to several factors, such as the global economic uncertainty caused by the COVID-19 pandemic, as well as the decrease in interest rates that made gold a more attractive investment option for big investors. The central banks of several countries, including the Federal Reserve, have implemented accommodative monetary policies, which have resulted in lower interest rates and increased demand for gold as an alternative investment. The global gold price in 2021 reached a new high, with prices consistently trending upward throughout the year. According to the data from the WGC, the average gold price in 2021 was around Rs 4,2750.1, a rise of almost 1 percent over the previous year. Additionally, low interest rates and fiscal stimulus measures implemented by central banks around the world also supported higher gold prices due to increased demand from China and other emerging markets where various investors turned to gold as safe asset to protect their wealth and mitigate risk. As these economies continued to grow, their demand for gold as an investment and store value also increased. In 2022, gold prices reached an all-time high, recording at Rs 45437.48, an increase of approximately 6 percent from the previous year. Overall, the gold price trend from 2018 to 2022 shows a steady upward trajectory, driven by a combination of economic, geopolitical and pandemic-related factors.

In addition to the spot price of gold,[16] there is also London Bullion Market Association (LBMA)[17] gold price and a range of regional/local gold prices. The various regional gold prices are significant for local markets, while the LBMA Gold Price serves as a significant benchmark for the global gold market. The present dynamics of supply and demand of global gold price are reflected in the spot price which is subject to daily, weekly, monthly and yearly fluctuations. It is essential to keep in mind that the spot price is distinct from the price that buyers or investors may pay for physical gold, which may be greater owing to things like production costs, shipping costs and dealer commissions.

G20 Countries Gold Reserve Holding

The quantity of gold owned by all central banks and governments worldwide is referred to as the global gold reserves. The world's gold reserves are difficult to estimate with exact precision since some countries do not make their gold holdings known to the public. However, the WGC estimates that the total tonnes of gold held by Central banks until October 2022 (Q3) is 35,369.1 tonnes which is higher than the 31,192.50 tonnes held in Q4'2021. Table 1.6 shows a list of countries, their respective regions, economic groupings, the amount of gold in tonnes they hold in their reserves[18] and the percentage of their reserves that gold represents. The table illustrates the percentage of gold reserves held by each country in relation to the total gold reserves held by all the countries listed. For instance, the United States holds 66.7 percent of the total gold reserves held by the countries listed in the table. It is interesting to note that some countries with smaller absolute gold reserves, such as Turkey and Argentina, have a relatively high percentage of gold reserves compared to their total reserves. On the other hand, some countries with larger absolute gold reserves, such as Russia and China, have a relatively lower percentage of gold reserves. This suggests that the proportion of gold reserves a country hold is not necessarily correlated with the size of its economy or the absolute amount of its gold reserves. The United States, Germany, Italy, France,

Table 1.6 Global Gold Holding of G20 Countries

Countries	Region	Economic Grouping	Tonnes	Percent of Reserve
United States	North America	High income	8,133.5	66.7%
Germany	Western Europe	High income	3,355.1	65.9%
Italy	Western Europe	High income	2,451.8	63.2%
France	Western Europe	High income	2,436.8	58.4%
Russia	Central and Eastern Europe	Upper middle income	2,298.5	20.6%
China	East Asia	Upper middle income	1,980.3	3.4%
Japan	East Asia	High income	846.0	3.9%
India	**South Asia**	**Lower middle income**	**786.3**	**8.0%**
Turkey	Central and Eastern Europe	Upper middle income	517.0	26.9%
European Central Bank (ECB)	European Union	–	504.8	29.4%
Saudi Arabia	Middle East and North Africa	High income	323.1	3.8%
United Kingdom	Western Europe	High income	310.3	10.1%
Brazil	Latin America and Caribbean	Upper middle income	129.7	2.2%
South Africa	Sub-Saharan Africa	Upper middle income	125.4	11.8%
Mexico	Latin America and Caribbean	Upper middle income	119.9	3.3%
Republic of Korea	East Asia	High income	104.4	1.4%
Australia	Australasia/ Oceania	High income	79.8	7.8%
Indonesia	South East Asia	Upper middle income	78.6	3.4%
Argentina	Latin America and Caribbean	Upper middle income	61.7	9.1%

Source: World Gold Council, World Official Gold Holdings, International Financial Statistics, January 2023.

Russia, China and India are the top eight G20 countries in terms of gold reserves. These eight countries hold 90.44 percent of over 22,288.30 tonnes of gold which is more than other twelve G20 countries, with the highest 66.7 percent of reserve in gold by the United States. Even the European Central bank (ECB) holds more quantity of gold when compared with the United Kingdom. This is due to the fact that the central bank of the United Kingdom is primarily concerned with their domestic economy and the stability of national currency (pound).

India, even though a lower middle-income country, still holds a higher amount of gold when compared with other twelve G20 countries.

This is because India has a substantial and well-established jewellery industry, which supports the nation's overall demand for gold. The government of India has implemented policies that promote the use of gold as a store of value and investment, such as the Gold Monetization Scheme as mentioned earlier, which enables households to deposit their gold with the government for interest payments. The Economic Times stated on January 12, 2023, that the amount of gold imported in December 2022 was 79 percent lower than in December 2021. This decrease in imports for the second-largest gold consumer in the world might cap increases in the trading of gold prices globally. Because of this, RBI has increased its gold holdings to diversify its foreign reserve through several ways: a) by making direct purchases of gold from the international market – these purchases are made through IMF or from other countries' central banks; b) by joining into gold swap agreement with other countries' central banks. This agreement allows RBI to trade gold for its foreign currency holdings with another central bank; c) one more service provided by the RBI is the easing of gold imports into India, which increases the RBI's foreign exchange reserves. This has led to an increasing demand for gold in India, and the country is now one of the world's largest consumers of gold.

Gold is one of the most valuable precious metals in the world. From jewellery to bullion coins, gold has been used for centuries as a symbol of wealth, prosperity and power. As we have shown, consumption of gold continues to grow globally as it is driven by a variety of factors, including culture, economics and investment.

Notes

1 The gold standard established a connection between a nation's holdings of gold and the quantity of money it could issue by allowing its currency to be convertible into gold at a set rate. Because it gave the value of money a concrete and limited foundation, using gold as a standard helped to stabilise currency values and avoid inflation.

2 'Under the classic gold standard, this would have caused an outflow of gold from the United States, a fall in the money supply, and a return of the dollar's buying power to its official gold price. Meanwhile, the United States was getting closer to the legal limit on currency that could be outstanding on the gold stock that was held in reserve' (Elwell, 2011).

3 To manage the crisis in 1991, the State Bank of India was given a lease on 20 tonnes of gold from the government's stock to permit it to sell gold overseas with the option to buy it back after six months in order to avoid a balance of payment failure. The Government of India endorsed the July shipment of 47 tonnes of gold to the Bank of England by the Reserve Bank of India. This assisted in raising $600 million in the United Sttaes. In July 1991, the rupee's currency rate was changed to bring it to a level that could be sustained in global market. These examples demonstrate the IMF and India's successful relationship (Srinivas, 2019, p. 75).

4 The process of converting gold bullion into semi-finished or finished jewellery is known as jewellery fabrication. This is different from jewellery consumption in that it doesn't include makers' and distributors' stock building and de-stocking activities. Additionally, it does not include imports or exports at the national level. Supply and Demand Notes and Definition, World Gold Council, 2022.

5 'Market Analysis of North American Gold Jewelry Market', https://www.levinsources.com/assets/listings/Jewelry-North-America_Zahabu-Safi-Clean-Gold.pdf

6 The entire quantity of gold invested in bars and coins as well as the amount of gold consumed in jewellery inside a nation, expressed in fine weight. As technology demand is assessed at the point of fabrication rather than consumption, it is not taken into account at the level of each particular country. Supply and Demand Notes and Definition https://www.gold.org/goldhub/research/jewellery-demand-and-trade-india-gold-market-series#chart1

7 Reserve Bank of India, Annual Report 2020–21, p 89.

8 The term 'year-over-year' refers to comparing information or occurrences from one calendar year to the same time the year before.

9 Jewellery demand and trade: India gold market series, January 19, 2023, https://www.gold.org/goldhub/research/jewellery-demand-and-trade-india-gold-market-series

10 Explained | What is gold recycling? The Hindu, June 26, 2022 07:44 pm; https://www.thehindu.com/business/Industry/explained-what-is-gold-recycling/article65560282.ece

11 Jewellery demand and trade: India gold market series, January 19, 2013, https://www.gold.org/goldhub/research/jewellery-demand-and-trade-india-gold-market-series

12 Focus 1: Growth of organised recycling in India, https://www.gold.org/goldhub/research/gold-refining-and-recycling-india-gold-market-series

13 A weaker dollar was the dominant contributor to Gold's positive return in December, January 9, 2023, https://www.gold.org/goldhub/research/gold-market-commentary-december-2022

14 The Intercontinental Exchange (ICE) subsidiary known as the ICE Benchmark Administration (IBA) is in charge of managing benchmark for several financial markets, including commodities, interest rates and stocks as well as including risk management and investment choices.

15 The Intercontinental Exchange (ICE) subsidiary known as the ICE Benchmark Administration (IBA) is in charge of managing benchmark for several financial markets, including commodities, interest rates and stocks as well as including risk management and investment choices.

16 The current market price for a troy ounce of gold (31.1034768 grams) is referred to as the 'spot price' for gold and is often given in US dollars. Traders, investors and other market players purchase, sell and assess the current value of the asset using the spot price.

17 It is a global trade organisation that represent the gold and silver bullion market that support diversified gold market by including the gold holding central bank, as well as investors from private banks, mining firms, refiners and manufacturer. https://www.lbma.org.uk/publications/the-otc-guide/frequently-asked-questions

18 Central Bank Data, 2023 – https://www.gold.org/goldhub/data/gold-reserves-by-country.

2 Kaleidoscopic View of Indian Gold Jewellery

Tracing the History, Culture and Beauty

Material Culture: Gold Jewellery

'Jewellery' as a cultural entity has led to the diffusion and creation of patterned tradition since ages in India. It is a symbol of cultural transmission of artefacts that captures the essence of our assimilated multi-cultural heterogeneous India. It refers to a variety of things customised for personal ornaments, decorations and priceless items for self-adornment and beautification. Indian literary and archaeological pieces based on texts and visual arts provide evidence that gold jewellery has enchanted people for its rarity and appealing colour from pre-historic times (B & T, 1990; Smith, 1908; Krishnan & Kumar, 1999, p. 266). People wear gold for ornamentation and decoration of various material objects like clothes, utensils, architecture, sculpture, ritualistic articles and paintings. Gold also serves as a medium of exchange as gold coins, as well as a source of medicine and adornment.

It has continued to be a popular material because of its clarity, robustness and simplicity – qualities that have given it a consistent value since time immemorial. Indian Vedic literature and verses have repeatedly emphasised the usefulness of gold in Indian society and culture, a fact that is underscored by B.N. Mukherjee's research on gold coins in the Rig Vedic literature. He suggested that the use of gold in India dates to the second millennium B.C. and is a testimonial to gifts of 'hundred *niska*'. The term *niska* refers to 'gold ornament'. It is a means of purification, and immortal life, and is used for many auspicious rites. For these aspects, we use gold in jewellery for protection against negativity and the evil eye. Archaeological sources, geological data, ethnographic studies and literary evidence all show that the Indian context strongly connects ecology and technology (Nanda, 1992, p. 195), with people frequently using gold metal as jewellery and ornaments to maintain socio-cultural, religious and economic stability. Archaeological sources provide tangible evidence of the craftsmanship, intricate designs and cultural significance of gold jewellery throughout different historical

DOI: 10.4324/9781032717951-2

periods. The study of geological data sheds light on the geological formations and deposits that contribute to the availability and distribution of gold, further emphasising its importance in Indian material culture. Ethnographic studies offer valuable insights into the social and cultural contexts in which gold jewellery is used, highlighting its role as a symbol of social status, religious devotion and cultural identity. Additionally, literary evidence enriches our understanding of the cultural practices, religious rituals and economic transactions associated with gold jewellery. By considering the material culture of gold jewellery, we gain a deeper appreciation for its significance as a tangible expression of Indian cultural heritage. The intricate craftsmanship, symbolism and social functions of gold jewellery highlight its central role in shaping and preserving the material culture of India.

Selected Indian Legends: Relevance of Gold Jewelleries

India has been referred to as a 'bird of gold' or '*sone ki chidiya*' for its resources which include vast geographical areas with varied climates, vegetation, minerals, communities and cultures. Gold has been a prominent feature of precious metals/stones since ancient times, and it continues to be a versatile medium for a wide range of gold jewellery designs that cater to specific cultural preferences. These designs may include embedded gems, stones or other metals, and the demand for such jewellery remains strong in the present day. Indian mythology provides a strong link to the socio-religious and cultural significance of gold jewellery which is reflected in the Vedas, Ramayana, Mahabharata, Buddhism, Jainism and other literature. Thomas Holbein Hendley mentioned the correlation between Indian legends and gold jewellery in the book *Indian Jewelleries*, which provides rich information on how gold jewellery symbolically plays an important role in Indian culture and society. There are numerous references in Indian mythology and legends. A few examples where gold jewellery has been referred to in the legends are provided here:

- One legend is the tale of *Shakuntala*, a beautiful woman who secretly married *King Dushyanta*. He gave her a gold ring, intricately engraved with King Dushyanta's name, as a symbol of their love and commitment. One day sage *Durvasas* cursed *Shakuntala* that the man (husband) whom she loves will forget her because she failed to greet him (Durvasas) properly. Because of the curse, she misplaced the gold ring while bathing in the sacred river Ganga, which was a symbol of love and marriage. As a result, *King Dushyanta* had forgotten about their marriage and she did not have any proof of their wedding to show him. So, *Shakuntala* was compelled to leave the palace and went back to her father's ashram. The curse was to be lifted when *King Dushyanta* would see the gold ring, he had given her. Finally, the gold ring was found in the belly of a fish. When the King finally noticed the gold ring, his memory was restored. The story indicates the power of a material object such as a gold ring which holds emotional significance.

• Lord Krishna is often depicted wearing various types of gold jewellery which have different symbolic meanings – such as wearing of *Vaijanti Mala and gold armlets*. *Vaijanti Mala* is made of gold and precious stones. In a kirtan (devotional song), Lord Krishna's adornment is beautifully described as, '*Mayura Mukut Pitambar Sohe, Gale Vaijanti Mala* (The golden peacock crown shines brightly, and around the neck there is a garland made of *Vaijanti* beads crafted from gold)'. We believe it is an element of opulence and beauty of sacred gold metal that symbolises Krishna's strength over negative energies and evil power.

• The golden deer is a symbol of immense wealth and pleasure in Hindu mythology. Sita, the bride of Lord Rama, is kidnapped in the epic Ramayana by King Ravana, who sent a mystical golden deer to divert Lord Rama and his brother Lakshmana. According to the legend, the golden deer was decked with gold jewellery, including a necklace, earrings and other accessories. While she was being taken away by King Ravana, she deliberately dropped her gold jewellery from the chariots as a sign for Lord Rama and Lakshmana to find her. It served as a symbolic clue for Lord Rama. Gold jewellery is often used as a resource in difficult situations.

• According to the Legends, young *Kunti* was given a mantra by sage *Durvasas*, who said that it would enable her to call upon any deity she desired to have a child with. Young *Kunti*, who was curious, summoned Lord Surya (the sun god), to test the mantra. Lord Karna was born with golden armour and earrings attached to his body. It is a symbol of royal lineage and his connection to the sun god. The golden armour represented his invincibility and impenetrability in battle, offering him protection from harm. And his gold earring was believed to enhance his perception and intuition, enabling him to make wise and strategic decisions on the battlefield. Gold jewellery symbolised his exceptional strength, resilience and the divine favour bestowed upon him.

• Other than these, *Rukmini* – wife of Lord Krishna is the incarnation of the goddess Lakshmi (goddess of wealth and prosperity). She was known for her gold jewellery worn at the time of her wedding. She wore a set of jewellery made of gold studded with gemstones, diamonds, emeralds and rubies. And this has become an inspiration for Indian women to adorn gold jewellery on their wedding day.

• Lord Krishna and Sudama were childhood friends, but they eventually went their separate ways as adults. One day, Sudama went to see Lord Krishna. He had a bowl of flattened rice with him which he intended to offer as a gift to his old friend but he was ashamed of his poverty. When Lord Krishna heard of Sudama's visit, he perceived the true value of Sudama's gift, which had been extended with love and admiration. In return, therefore, Lord Krishna gave him a generous gift of gold jewellery. It serves as a symbolic representation of the intense sacred relationship between the two individuals.

• Temple jewellery is typically made of gold and is adorned with intricate designs including images of deities – especially Lord Shiva, Lord Ganesh, Goddess Lakshmi, mythical creatures and other traditional motifs. Temple jewellery is a sort of customary South Indian adornment that is frequently connected to classical dance genres like Bharatanatyam, Kuchipudi and Mohiniattam. During religious rituals and festivals, temple-goers frequently wear these specific types of jewellery. Wearing temple jewellery is said to establish a connection with the divine. The temple jewellery's depictions of gods and goddesses and other holy symbols are thought to be a means of calling upon the divine power and getting gods' and goddesses' favours.

Overall, these stories highlight the cultural significance of gold jewellery in mythology and folklore and how it is often associated with belief systems.

Gold Jewellery Connoisseurs in India: A Legacy of an Era

The Archaeological Survey of India has been conducting research at Rakhi Garhi, a hamlet in the Hisar region of Haryana, for the past 32 years. This site is a part of the Indus Valley Civilization from where gold jewellery was discovered, according to an article published in India Today on May 8, 2022. References from Shatapatha Brahmana provide detailed descriptions of gold jewellery elements found in the epics Ramayana and Mahabharata, which made gold jewellery popular among people living in India. This popularity had increased because of its sacredness (Nanda, 1992) which is associated with immortality, purity and being the protector against evil. For Indians, gold jewellery is associated with religious beliefs, rites and ceremonies. It is a sacred element that makes everything 'pure' as this 'gold' metal does not change its nature. It is associated with ten synonyms in Sanskrit language which are *Swarna, suvarna, hiranya, kanak, kanchan, hem, ashtapada, chandra, jatarapa* and *harita* (Bhattacharya, 2002, Nanda, 1992). Wearing gold as earrings, necklaces, forehead rings and other adornments (Jha, 2004) had a customary usage from the Classical Indian era. An in-depth observation of gold jewellery provides insight into the legacy of the Indian era and its relevance in contemporary India.

India, one of the world's oldest civilisations, has a long history of using and mining gold. Gold was found in forms of jewellery, especially from Mohenjodaro, Harappa and Lothal, as well as from other auriferous deposits from Karnataka (Kolar, Hutti, Anantapur, Gadag town in Hampi), Tamil Nadu (Wyanad), Andhra Pradesh, Bihar, Gujarat, Kerala. Kautilya has mentioned that the availability of gold was found in various parts of Indian mines, rivers and mountains and 'it was imported from south India into the Indus cities ... there is evidence to suggest that *lac* occurs even in the jewellery of the Indus Valley' (Krishnan & Kumar, 1999, p. 267). Using gold objects as jewellery and other personal adornments has been described in Rajini Nanda's book *The Early History of Gold in India* and other archaeological data.

The usage of gold ornaments was not utilised by all Indian Chalcolithic societies because the usage of gold varied according to areas, cultural traditions and customs. In Rajasthan, Gilund was the site of the discovery of gold jewellery – as beads, pendants and earrings. The lost-wax casting method was used to create these jewelleries, which entails modelling the pieces of jewelleries in wax and then casting it in gold, crafted with meticulous precision, emerged through the intricate wire drawing process – a technique where a thread of gold is delicately pulled through a drawplate, transforming it into a slender strand fit for the creation of exquisite jewellery. Notably, in the state of Karnataka, the archaeological site of Dharwar bore witness to the discovery of captivating gold ornaments, unravelling a chapter of the past.

Delving further into annals of history, Indian Megalithic societies of the first millennium BCE unveil a striking affinity for gold jewellery, permeating both the Northern and Southern regions of India. Archival evidence sheds light on the staggering abundance of gold beads and ornaments discovered in the Madurai and Chingleput districts of Tamil Nadu. The Adichanallur district, on the other hand, revealed a captivating glimpse of gold leaf and ribbons fashioned into resplendent diadems and pendants. Meanwhile, the Nagarjunakonda district unveiled a captivating spiral-shaped earring, meticulously crafted using a string of gleaming golden beads. Gold beads as earrings were unearthed in Jammu and Kashmir. In the second millennium BCE[1] in Maharashtra, gold ornaments were excavated from Daimabad and a gold necklace was excavated in Nagpur, Mahurjhari people once wore thin gold-wire necklaces with pendants in the shapes of spirals or rectangles made of gold strips fashioned like leaves along with gold earring founded by the archaeologists. Additionally, the horse emerged as the foremost and beloved domesticated animal during the megalithic era, leaving an indelible mark on the cultural landscape. Evidence of this bond between humans and horses can be seen in the discovery of gold ornaments specifically crafted for these majestic creatures at the renowned megalithic site of Vidarbha. Moreover, the widespread presence of gold mines, notably in Kolar and Hutti, attests to the immense significance placed on this precious metal. These abundant sources of gold not only fuelled the creation of captivating jewellery but also contributed to the flourishing trade and economic prosperity of ancient Indian societies. These intertwined threads of gold, horses and thriving gold mines weave a captivating narrative, unravelling the splendour and grandeur of megalithic India, where gold reigned supreme, both as a symbol of status and as a testament to the artistic expertise of a civilisation engraved in time.

India's historical landscape gleams with a legacy of gold discoveries. Among them, the Indus Valley Civilization (2700–1900 BC) stands as a pioneering civilisation, being one of the earliest in the world to embrace and utilise the allure of gold. This period in India's history also boasts a vibrant tapestry of gold mining, weaving together a rich narrative of prosperity and reverence for this precious metal. At Mohenjodaro, gold was manufactured for the creation of various types of personal pieces of jewellery as *gold beads* (made of two circular sections that were gold soldered together and grooved in the middle to create threading holes), *gold bracelets* (made up of loose small-sized gold beads threaded in six rows and the gold terminals at the end of the bracelets were hollow, flattened and semi-circular), *gold necklace* (made up of small, globular and cylindrical beads combined with steatite beads), *gold pendant* (made up of gold and sky-blue coloured glaze), *gold fillets* (made up of very thin gold wire of 0.4 inches for nose or forehead jewellery), a *gold band* (made up of gold fillet having 6.2 inches by 0.75 inches), *gold bangles* (made of a hollow gold tube filled with *lac*), etc.

At Harappa, huge collections of gold jewellery pieces were discovered by the Indian archaeologists which included: a *gold sheet armlet* with a hollow interior and tapering edges on both sides, *cone-shaped forehead gold jewellery* worn over the braid of hair from the forehead to the top of the head-dress, a *heart-shaped gold pendant* (made by three beaten gold sheets from the behind in a shape of three concentric heart-shaped design), *gold brooch* used as dress pin and hairpin, *gold wristlets*, several designs of *gold necklaces*, *gold nose ring and pendants,* and *gold beads* for making jewellery of several objects and animal figures, Gold-coated terracotta beads ornaments were excavated in Meerut and Uttar Pradesh[2] and *gold leaf-designed* objects used for making jewellery were found in Sahiwal and Punjab. Rajasthani *Borla* is influenced by Indus Valley sheet gold forehead ornaments. At Chanhudaro, gold foil wrapped in bangles made of copper beads were found. At Lothal (presently in Ahmadabad Gujarat), gold pendant, gold nose rings, gold earrings and gold beads were used for making a gold necklace.

Rig Veda is one of the oldest sacred texts of Hinduism that provides some insights into the usage and types of gold jewellery during that time. The *Rig Veda* text claims that gold jewellery was worn by both males and females for ornamentation and religious purposes,[3] and it was used as a sign of wealth[4] and a symbol of social status. The text refers to several different kinds of gold jewellery, including anklets, armlets, bracelets and necklaces. Other things, including chariots and idols, were also embellished with gold. One hymn, for instance, describes gold as being used to buy a cow, while another describes it as being used to pay for goods and services. The Shatapatha Brahmana, a Vedic text from circa 800 BCE, discusses priests wearing gold jewellery while performing religious ceremonies and also provides information about the jewellery worn by the monarchs and other rulers. Moreover, the customs of exchanging jewellery at the time of a wedding found deep roots in Vedic times (Krishnan & Kumar, 1999, p. 58). These glimpses of the past illuminate the profound significance of gold jewellery in both religious and societal realms during this era.

The mention of gold jewellery in the scriptures was written by both Buddhists and Jain serves as a testament to the deep-rooted veneration for this precious metal across a multitude of religious traditions. The Buddhist doctrine of Dhamma states that monks and nuns are not allowed to wear any jewellery when they are in retreat or when they are meditating because, in their view, to earn eternal salvation, one should give up all material possessions and contemporary life's joys. They view gold as a representation of the sun and fire, which they associate with wisdom, holiness, joy and freedom. However, when gold is combined with other metals like copper, bronze or silver to make jewellery, the purity of the gold is contaminated. As a result, gold is only utilised in Buddhist art; it is not used in jewellery.

Pendants worn by the Buddhists have some specific symbolic religious designs tied/painted with gold; such symbols are pairs of Gold Fish that symbolise overcoming difficulties; Gold Lotus Fish that symbolises the attainment of the cleanliness of body, verbal communication and mind free from negativity; and Gold *Dharma Chakra* that symbolises avoiding indulgences. During the reign of Lord Buddha, all sections of people were hierarchically segregated and placed based on their caste structure possessing gold jewellery with the symbols mentioned earlier. Even the Buddhist Ajanta cave paintings feature characters bearing jewellery that has an attractive appearance. Female figures painted specifically in the Buddhist Cave XVII are depicted completely adorned in jewellery and demonstrating the significance of this form of art. In the Jaina Agamas, the terms *hara* (a necklace with nine strings), *egavali* (a necklace with one string), *muttavali* (a pearl necklace), *kanagavali* (a gold necklace), *palamba* (a neck covering), *kadi* (a waist ornament), *kadagai* (bangles), *tundiyai* (armlets), *keurai* (a bracelet) and *chudamani* (a head ornament) have all been mentioned. Elephants and horses were also given ornaments made of gold and valuable stones in addition to men and women.

Steeped in the realms of antiquity, the Maurya empire (321–185 BC) rises with resplendent glory, celebrated for its opulent cultural heritage and remarkable contributions to the realm of jewellery design. Their empire's rich artistic heritage and skilled craftsmanship have continued to be admired and appreciated for their beauty and intricate designs. Gold jewellery, a symbol of opulence and prestige, held immeasurable value during this era. The jewellery of this period was distinguished by its complex patterns and meticulous craftsmanship, with the use of a variety of methods – including casting, filigree, granulation and repousse. The usage of animal motifs, such as elephants (utilised as symbols of strength and power), lions (a symbol of courage and bravery as it is connected with the deity Vishnu) and peacocks (frequently used to represent study, wisdom, art and learning as it is associated with goddesses Saraswati), were thought to have sacred significance. These patterns were frequently used to create necklaces, bracelets, armlets, earrings and rings which were some of the fashionable jewellery pieces. The process of granulation, in which tiny gold beads are fused to form complex patterns, was frequently utilised to produce these motifs and designs.

Another well-known method was called filigree, which included twisting and forming tiny gold wires into beautiful designs. Pearls, diamonds, rubies and emeralds were among the valuable and semi-precious stones frequently used in Mauryan jewellery. These stones were regularly utilised to accentuate the beauty of the jewellery in sophisticated designs, such as floral and geometric patterns. Wearing gold jewellery every day and for customary practice increased in the post-Maurya period with its distinctive designs and tastes. While some people chose simple, beautiful designs, others opted for ornate, highly detailed jewellery. The Satavahanas were widely known for their love of gold jewellery which was frequently intricately carved and set with valuable stones. The Kushanas were recognised for producing magnificent gold coins with images of the monarchs and their families. They also wore gold jewellery, which frequently featured pearls and other jewels, such as finger rings, bracelets, earrings and necklaces. The Gupta and Chola kingdoms loved wearing gold jewellery with ornate decorations and patterns (for example design of lion-head images in bracelet designs). The Cholas held a monopoly over gold mines and pearl fisheries showing their extensive taste for jewellery. The repertoire of Chola jewellery showcases at least 65 different kinds of ornaments. For example, flat collar necklaces or *Karai* were made of gold sheet embellished with gems and crocodile-shaped ear ornament, and waistband/chain was made of gold flower sets with diamond/precious gems. Moreover, pure gold without any alloys was used to create the decorations and with the use of gold embroidery on silk fabric – the robe became an ornament by itself. The enduring legacy of their exquisite jewellery creations resonates through the ages, forever enchanting the hearts of art and jewellery enthusiasts across generations.

During ancient India's Sangam period, the significance of gold jewellery soared to remarkable heights, holding a pivotal role in the cultural fabric of the era. In this splendid epoch, women adorned themselves with exquisite gold jewellery, embellished with precious stones and adorned with intricate designs. Symbolising far more than mere adornment, these precious ornaments became a visual represen-tation of status and opulence. Affluent individuals proudly exhibited their rank and prosperity by adorning themselves with elaborate and valuable gold jewellery, further accentuating their elevated social standing. Gold jewellery was often exchanged as gifts between members of the royal family, nobility and wealthy merchants. These gifts were considered a symbol of generosity and friendship and were utilised in religious rites and ceremonies as offerings. Gold was used to decorate temples and shrines, and people frequently presented gold jewellery as a sign of their dedication and devoutness. The classical literary texts unveil a dazzling array of gold jewellery, each with its own distinctive name and purpose. Among them are *rumka* (gold chain or disc), *Ruchaka* (Gold necklace), *kataka* (gold bracelet), *kangavali* (jewellery for neck composed of gold coins and beads), *Manisopana* (gold chain made of beads), *kanaka kanchi/ Hemamekhala/ kanchi/ mekhela/kinkini/rasana* (a gold griddle), *chudamani* (jewellery for head), *kundela* (earring), etc. (Nanda, 1992, pp. 207, 208). These magnificent pieces of jewellery were often complemented with other precious substances such as pearls, rubies, corals, emeralds, diamonds and large gemstones, sourced predominantly from the town of Madurai, serving as the primary gemstone hub of the era.

The rule of prominent rulers and empires from the 14th century marked the second legacy of gold jewellery. Over time, the design of Indian gold jewellery became more intricate and ornate. During this era (1526–1857), gold jewellery became more elaborate and featured gem-stones and enamel. The Mughal emperors expressed their love of luxury and opulence by creating intricate and ornate designs for their jewellery.

The Delhi Sultanate was a Muslim empire that ruled over a significant portion of India from the 13th century to the 16th century. The Sultanate was established by the first Muslim ruler of India, Qutub-ud-din Aibak, in 1206, and the dynasty lasted until the Mughal conquest of India in the 16th century. Malik Kafur's expeditions in southern India resulted in the acquisition of vast riches through the plunder of gold jewellery during each invasion. Babur found the Mughal Empire in 1526 which lasted until the mid-19th century.

We know the Mughal emperors for their patronage of the arts, architecture, literature and music. Usha R. Bala Krishnan and Mira Sushil Kumar's book *Indian Jewellery: Dance of the Peacock* examines the extensive heritage of Mughal jewellery and how it has shaped Indian dance and culture. Mughal jewellery is well-known for its exquisite craftsmanship, intricate designs (inscribed spinel's) and the use of precious gemstones, especially jade. It was created using precious metals like gold and silver, and the artisans who crafted it were highly skilled in the art of jewellery making. The inclusion of rare and valuable jewels such as diamonds, emeralds, rubies and sapphires served to enhance the beauty and prestige of these magnificent pieces. Mughal emperors were avid art collectors who ordered extravagant jewellery sets for themselves and their queens, frequently combining Persian and European designs. The jewellery worn by dancers, including necklaces, earrings, bangles and anklets, is described in the book as being an essential component of their costumes. To convey the fluidity and movement of the dancers, they frequently made jewellery to match the hues and patterns of the costumes. The book also explores the symbolism of certain types of jewellery in Indian dance. For example, the *maang tikka* (a forehead ornament) represents the third eye and is believed to enhance the spiritual energy of the dancer. Female dancers portraying mythological characters often wear the *nath* (nose ring) to symbolise the power of the goddess.

During the long years of the Muslim dynasty, we have witnessed a hybridisation of Indo-Muslim ideas in gold jewellery art style. This amalgamation of designs and techniques of making jewellery by the Indian *swarnakars* (gold jewellery artisans) has provided unique and diverse styles in gold jewellery. Although Portuguese, French, Dutch and English migrated and dominated Indian society, they were unable to influence Indian gold jewellery crafting styles, designs, beliefs and sentiments attached to gold. Therefore, with an increase in the domination of the colonial rules, the art forms in jewellery designs and patterns became hard to separate. For example, Mughal jewellery often featured intricate floral designs and delicate filigree work that was influenced by Hindu traditions. At the same time, Mughal jewellery also incorporated Islamic motifs, such as the crescent moon and stars, which were often used in necklaces, earrings and other pieces. These are just a few of the major dynasties and empires that ruled over India during the medieval period. The period was characterised by a complex interplay of different cultures, religions and political systems, which has left a rich and diverse legacy that continues to influence India to this day. A synthesis action and assimilation of Muslim artwork (with more Arabic and less Persian influence) and Hindu artwork has mesmerised the eyes of the people living in India and the travellers. They adhered to the original artwork and created new forms in old kinds of designs to give jewellery a fresh look and pattern, such as *kanphool jhumkas* made of *kundan* and *guluband*. During this time, animal figures became more prevalent and were used as symbols of religion or belief in jewellery along with floral and faunal motifs. Similarly, engraving of elephant heads, peacock heads with beaks and eyes, peacock tails, lion heads and fish forms, and sun, moon, crescent and stars symbols, were found in jewellery.

A grand South Indian empire was established in the year 1344 known as the Vijayanagara Empire that existed until the 17th century. It was founded by the brothers Harihara and Bukka. Historical accounts suggest that Krishnadeva Raya and his queen were patrons of art and culture and contributed significantly to the prosperity of the Vijayanagara Empire. It is said that they supported the construction of grand temples such as Hazara Rama Temple, the Vithala Temple and the Kodandarama Temple; according to a myth golden cows and chariots studded with gems and gold ornaments were gifted to Tirupati. One notable form of gold jewellery found in the Vijayanagara Empire was the 'Manga Malai' or mango-shaped necklace. This exquisite piece consisted of intricately designed gold mango motifs linked together to form a stunning adornment for the neck. The craftsmanship displayed in these necklaces showcased the empire's mastery of goldsmithing techniques. In addition to these, the Vijayanagara Empire was known for its gold armlets, waistbelts, intricate nose rings and extravagant hair ornaments, all crafted with meticulous attention to detail and artistic flair.

The Maratha Empire was a Hindu empire that ruled over large parts of India from the 17th century to the early 19th century. The empire was founded by Shivaji, and it was known for its guerrilla warfare tactics and its military strength. During the Shivaji era, gold jewellery was frequently handcrafted and engraved with elaborate designs, including floral patterns, geometric forms and conventional themes like peacocks and elephants. The designs were often created by local art and architecture. Shivaji was a devout Hindu, and his association with gold jewellery and designs often encompasses religious elements. Designs may include sacred Hindu symbols such as Om, *trishul* (trident) or lotus, reflecting the religious beliefs and devotion of Shivaji and his followers. Those designs may incorporate motifs or symbols associated with Shivaji's military prowess, such as swords, shields or crowns, regional symbol or emblem, representing his status as a noble and courageous leader. One notable feature of gold jewellery in his period was the use of large-sized gemstones, particularly diamonds. The use of diamonds in jewellery reflected the wealth and prosperity of the time, as well as the importance of luxury and prestige. Enamel work involved adding coloured glass to the gold jewellery, while filigree work which involved twisting and weaving fine gold wire was used to create delicate patterns. Thus, the Shivaji period showcased not only the mastery of gold craftsmanship but also the artistic exploration of techniques such as enamel work and filigree. These exquisite creations stood as enduring testaments to the era's ingenuity and creative spirit, etching their place in the annals of gold jewellery history.

The 18th century witnessed a remarkable artistic evolution in jewellery across diverse regions, as Hindu Maharajas in Rajasthan, Punjab, Hyderabad and Central India, along with Muslim Nawabs and Rajas, especially in Murshidabad and Lucknow and other princely states, patronised and contributed to the flourishing traditions of gold jewellery. The Nizams of Hyderabad – reputed richest men from the early 18th century to the early 20th century – had popularised Nizam-styled jewellery design in India. The style was known for its elaborate and intricate designs of gold set with Burmese rubies and spinel, diamonds from Golconda mines (Jacob diamonds[5]), pearls from India and Basra and Colombian emeralds (59 karat is the largest one and 6.5 is the lowest). 'Jewels of the Nizam' is the first elaborate documentation by Usha R Bala Krishnan on collections of jewellery worn by the Nizams. Nizam jewellery was an amalgamation of the craftsmanship of different regions – including Deccani, Lucknavi and Rajasthani. Oshman Ali Khan who was the last Nizam of Hyderabad, held the title until Indian Independence in 1947. In 1945, he assigned 107 personal jewellery items, including state insignia, to his grandsons and granddaughter. This act of assigning personal jewellery to his descendants indicates a transfer of ownership and inheritance within the Nizam's family. He created 'H.E.H. The Nizam's Jewellery Trust' on February 28th, 1956 and Supplemental Trust to preserve and protect the vast collection of their hereditary jewellery. Both trusts make up worth over 500 million dollars of the jewellery treasury of Hyderabad and gemstones. According to the Supreme Court decision of September 1979, the Government of India ordered that the gems of the Nizam were 'art treasures and in national interest they should not be permitted to be transported out of the country' (Krishnan, 2001). The Antiquities Act was further changed to allow for the forced acquisition of the remaining items of jewellery by designating them as 'art treasures'. The designs of Nizam-style jewellery were often inspired by traditional Indian motifs such as lotus, rose jasmine flowers, vine leaves and peacocks crafted using gold and precious gemstones. The popular technique involved setting gemstones into a gold frame using a type of wax for a smooth and seamless design, with no visible settings for Kundan jewellery; and for Jadau jewellery, uncut diamonds or polki diamonds were set and arranged into an irregular pattern of a gold frame that creates a unique and rustic look. Thus, Nizam-style jewellery is characterised by exquisite chokers and necklaces, which are crafted using multiple strands of gemstones and diamonds. Those designs typically exhibit a symmetrical and harmonious arrangement, lending an opulent and refined appearance to the jewellery.

Maharaja Sawai Jai Singh II, ruler of Kachwaha who ruled Jaipur from 1699 to 1743, was a patron of the arts and was well-known for encouraging the jewellery-making industry in Jaipur. He encouraged the expansion of the jewellery-making trade and supported skilled traditional jewellery artisans. Under his patronage, the city became known for jewellery craftsmanship and created beautifully intricate jewellery designs. Jaipur-styled gold jewellery is made by carefully twisting, bending and shouldering thin strands of gold wire. The city is renowned for its gemstone trade and has been a hub for gem cutting, polishing and trading for centuries. The availability of a wide range of precious and semi-precious gemstones, including rubies, emeralds and sapphires, allowed Jaipur jewellers to create stunning and vibrant designs. The technique often incorporates floral motifs, geometric patterns or scenes from mythology, resulting in visually stunning and colourful jewellery – such as bell-shaped *jhumkas* (earrings) and *Navratna* jewellery. *Navratna* is a combination of nine gemstones representing the nine celestial bodies in Vedic astrology where these nine gemstones are set in a specific arrangement, with each stone representing a particular planet. The arrangement and alignment of the gemstones create a unique pattern that is both meaningful and visually appealing. Jaipur jewellers are known for their creativity in cutting gemstones into unique shapes and patterns. They go beyond traditional cuts and explore innovative techniques to bring out the best in each gemstone. This results in distinctively shaped gemstones that add an element of uniqueness to the jewellery designs. These unconventional cuts and patterns contribute to the global recognition and exclusivity of Jaipur jewellery. Jaipur jewellery was worn in turban, sleeves and belts.

The Indian jewellery business saw tremendous upheaval during the 18th and 19th centuries. New jewellery styles and techniques emerged as a result of the blending of European styles (cherub and angel motifs) and techniques with traditional jewellery designs. A laurel wreath, a symbol of victory, was incorporated into necklaces, earrings and bracelets frequently made of gold leaves and beads. To add colour and texture to Indian jewellery, roses, which were a popular flower in Europe during the 19th century, were included. They were frequently represented in gold and occasionally they were adorned with priceless gems like rubies or diamonds. During the 20th century, Indian jewellery reflected the broader global preferences of the era renowned western jeweller Jacques Cartier became a favourite among Indian royals, who commissioned Cartier to create some of the most lavish and iconic jewellery pieces in history, including the famous Patiala necklace. This partnership between Cartier and Indian craftsmen and Maharajas helped to establish the brand's reputation as a purveyor of luxury jewellery to the world's elite. This fusion of Indian and Western design aesthetics led to the emergence of a distinctive style that continues to inspire contemporary jewellery makers.

During the colonial period in India, there were several influences on the evolution of Indian jewellery. The Portuguese introduced enamel work, which became popular among Indian jewellery makers and was incorporated into the local craft. The British colonial officials encouraged the use of diamonds and other precious stones in a more European style of jewellery-making, leading to the development of a unique Indo-European style. Additionally, the introduction of machine-made jewellery provided affordable and accessible options for consumers. Despite these foreign influences, Indian jewellery makers showcased their adaptability by incorporating these new styles into their existing craft, resulting in the creation of unique and beautiful jewellery pieces. The evolution of Indian jewellery over time reflects the cultural exchange and assimilation that occurred during the colonial period in India.

After India gained independence in 1947, a significant change in gold jewellery design was the transition from bulky, extravagant patterned jewellery towards lighter, more delicate designs that were easier to wear on a daily basis. This shift in design was driven by the increasing participation of women in the workforce, who required jewellery that was both practical and fashionable. This trend was also driven by the need for affordability and accessibility, as gold jewellery became more widely available and affordable to a larger population. Another trend that was eventually created was the increase in the popularity of diamond jewellery, which was viewed as a more cutting-edge replacement for traditional gold jewellery.

The 1990s saw a further shift towards contemporary styles of gold jewellery, with a focus on minimalism and simplicity. As a result, traditional designs such as heavy necklaces and bangles gave way to lighter, more delicate pieces that could be worn with both traditional and modern outfits. The demand for cut-and-polished diamonds increased significantly, and India became one of the world's largest suppliers. Modern gold jewellery designs are still a favourite among Indian women today and are frequently viewed as a sign of elegance and a symbol of style. Despite these changes, Indian consumers continue to choose traditional gold jewellery styles such as temple jewellery and vintage designs. These fashions are worn at special occasions like weddings and festivals and are frequently viewed to reconnect with India's rich cultural legacy. In post-independence India, gold jewellery styles, designs and patterns have continued to evolve, embracing both traditional heritage and modern influences. This dynamic mix has allowed for a diverse and vibrant range of gold jewellery options that often feature sleek and minimalist patterns, geometric shapes and fusion of materials, catering to the evolving tastes, occasions and preferences of a younger genera-tion. Additionally, an inclination towards fusion and experimentation in gold jewellery reflects a desire to break free from conventional norms and create distinctive, personalised pieces that cater to individual tastes and preferences. It allows for the exploration of diverse design possibili-ties and encourages innovation within the Indian gold jewellery industry.

The expansion of the large-scale gold jewellery industry resulted in the intensification of competition among capitalists. As capitalists sought to maximise their profits, they engaged in fierce competition, driving innovation and technological advancements. This competition was not limited to local or national markets but became universal in nature. The Indian diaspora spread across the globe plays a crucial role in driving the demand for Indian gold jewellery. Individuals of Indian origin seek to maintain their cultural connections and heritage by adorning themselves with traditional gold jewellery, fuelling the market demand in foreign countries.

The fundamental aspects of Indian jewellery, such as its types, designs and usages, have remained consistent over time despite changes in terminology. These enduring behaviours have been established as dynamic traditions in India and have persisted throughout the centuries. Today India continues to be a centre for conventional as well as contemporary gold jewellery. Even in contemporary times, it is difficult to distinguish whether a piece of jewellery is Mughal or Hindu style or a blend of various styles because of the high quality of craftsmanship. This speaks about the mastery and versatility of Indian jewellery makers in adapting and evolving their techniques over time.

Gold Jewellery: A Symbol of Beautification

Gold jewellery has been revered for its beauty and value for thousands of years, functioning as a symbol of wealth and prestige across cultures and countries. Beyond its social value, gold jewellery holds a particular belief in human culture as a means of decoration and self-expression. From delicate necklaces to loud designer pieces, gold jewellery can draw the viewer's attention and enhance the wearer's beauty. Whether it is a treasured family heirloom or a new purchase, gold jewellery continues to be a highly desirable and sought-after accessory, providing a sense of satisfaction and pride to those who wear it. These body adornments provide men and women with a sense of stability, safety and self-assurance. The practice of men wearing gold jewellery fell out of favour as European culture developed in India. There has been a resurgence of men's gold jewellery in India in recent years. While it may not be as prevalent as it was before the influence of European culture, many men are now choosing to wear gold necklaces, bracelets and rings as a fashion statement or as a symbol of their wealth and status. This revival of interest is particularly evident among younger generations, who are embracing traditional designs and incorporating them into contemporary fashion trends.

Women's bodies in the 21st century 'had become a key site of political, cultural, social and economic intervention' (Hancock, Philp., et al., 2000:1). They are presented as cultural icons in a wide range of occupations, from housework to the beauty industry. Because of this, before getting married, young women are more concerned with their physical beauty and wear various forms of jewellery on different parts of their bodies that are connected to their 'women-self-image'. Women's self-image is influenced by attractiveness throughout their life (Turner, 1984). The media plays a significant role in influencing self-image, often objectifying women's bodies. In the context of consumerism, the use of women models in jewellery advertisements has become prevalent. These advertisements tend to portray women as decorative objects, emphasising the selection of jewellery for specific occasions and highlighting how ornaments can enhance women's beauty, intelligence and elegance. Such content reinforces societal notions of beauty and perpetuates the idea that women's worth is closely tied to their physical appearance. Society at large, and women in particular, value the beautification of the body through adorning jewellery (Raha, 2020, p. 226). The connection between women and jewellery is deeply ingrained, particularly in India, where women feel incomplete without it because it is associated with societal norms, customs and the prevailing symbolic structure of society. Indian society symbolically legitimised adornment of the body with jewellery for its specific religious-spiritual and scientific significance, such as the age-old tradition of tying the *mangalsutra* (a necklace consisting of black beads strung on a gold thread) as a means of signifying a woman's marital status and endowing her with social legitimacy.

This symbolic meaning of adorning jewellery varies from the wearer to the viewer and the jewellery maker. The jewellery's aesthetic appeal carries deeper messages that amplify a person's attractiveness (Ghurye, 1950: 105). Those who accessorise themselves with jewellery often do so to conform to socio-cultural norms, enhance their attractiveness for their sense of fulfilment and create a pleasing aesthetic impression for those around them. The observer's response to the wearer's jewellery may vary, as they may or may not appreciate the visual impact created by the adornment. The observer's reaction is typically intentional, although their expectations and actual impressions may not always align (Raha, 2020, p. 227). The media's representation of women plays a significant role in shaping women's perceptions of the ideal body for wearing certain types of jewellery, both in terms of physical character- istics and aesthetic qualities. In Freud's opinion, an erogenous zone in the body part piques men's interest in women's bodies and causes them to become sexually curious (Slade, 2017: 16; Freud, 1920: 33). Therefore, jewellery is the type of object that draws attention to the area of the body (the erogenous zone). One of the erogenous areas of the female body, for instance, is the neck. It has long served as a significant location for artistic and sensual communication. Necklaces convey elegance, money, power, connection, status, levels of resources and aspects of identity and place in terms of culture (Raha, 2020: 228). Women are driven to pursue an appearance of perfection, and they are often captivated by television and other media that feature idealised depictions of women. This is why women are typically cast in jewellery advertisements because they wear jewellery more frequently than men, and it accentuates their natural beauty (Raha, 2016).

Along with Hindu gods and goddesses, kings and queens in Indian epics had symbolically set a standard for genders, across classes and cultures, to use different jewellery in different observable parts of their bodies. Thus, gold jewellery shows sexuality, aesthetics, status, iden- tity, fantasy, religiosity, tradition and culture and many other dimen- sions, making up the essence of Indian society and culture. For example, since ancient times, there has been a whole body of beliefs associated with the use of gold jewellery. Women with pierced noses gave birth with less discomfort and would prevent women from becoming hypnotised because of its influence over brain waves. A nose ring was also thought to improve a woman's emotional, romantic and sexual appeal by preserving the well-being of her reproductive organs (Thakur, 2014). A waist chain or hip belt is believed to help a pregnant woman to have a healthy foetus and safe delivery; it also helps to woman remain slim and fit as it prevents the accumulation of extra fat in those parts of the body. Thus, gold jewellery is associated with a certain intimacy that may not be present in other metals.

In South India, an expected mother was made to wear a protective bangle made of gold or black thread. This bangle is believed to protect both the mother and the unborn child from negative energy and evil spirits. The use of gold in this protective bangle may also signify the importance of wealth and prosperity in ensuring a safe and healthy pregnancy. This practice reflects the deeply rooted cultural beliefs and customs in India, which attach great significance to the use of jewellery in various life events. Bourdieu's concept of cultural capital can be applied here, as this practice of wearing protective bangles is seen as a marker of cultural knowledge and adherence to traditional customs, which are valued in Indian society.

The art of jewellery-making in India is steeped in history, with techniques and traditions passed down from generation to generation. From the intricate designs of Mughal-style jewellery to the bold, colourful creations of various sites, Indian jewellery is known for its beauty and craftsmanship. It has a constant value attached to affect emotions (Milovanovic, 2018). With its rich cultural significance and timeless appeal, Indian jewellery continues to captivate and inspire people all over the world.

Notes

1 Ray and Mohanty. (2016). Ornaments from Early Iron Age Megalithic Culture of Vidarbha. Heritage: Journal of Multidisciplinary Studies in Archaeology. (4). 611–626
2 IAR 1958-59:52, Y. D. Sharma. ASI
3 The deity Agni is supposed to 'sit in the middle of the gold-coloured flames' and is characterised as 'shining like gold'. This shows that gold was utilised to make holy items and altars and was connected to the gods.
4 The Atharva Veda mentions that gold jewellery was presented as gifts on various occasions as well as utilised as money and a medium of exchange to pay for goods and services. One hymn has mentioned that gold jewellery is mentioned as a type of compensation for wrongs that have been committed by the culprit.
5 The diamond was initially mined in Golconda, India, a region known for creating some of the most renowned diamonds in the whole world. The Jacob Diamond is named after Scottish jeweller *Alexander Malcolm Jacob*, who bought it in the late 19th century. He learned crafting jewellery from Calcutta jewellery artisans. To increase its brightness, Jacob had the diamond cut and polished, making it one of the biggest and most expensive diamonds in the world at the time. It is cut in a conventional Indian technique and consists of 184.75 carats. It has been estimated to be worth up to $100 million today and is one of the biggest diamonds ever found in India.

3 Gold Jewellery Industry in India

Knowing the Known: *Swarnakars* or Gold Jewellery-makers

Jewellery making is an art, a craft that has been mastered by the craftsmen over the ages. It involves technology with ample provisions for continuity of traditional art-forms or designs, creativity or improvisation; and passing on of the skill from one generation to the next. Fabrication of jewellery is in the hands of the *sonar/swarnakar*, the name by which the traditional Indian jewellers are known, who put their art and skill into gold for making jewelleries and ornaments. Indian gold jewellery-making industry had reached an advanced level of quality from the 1st century AD. Gold jewellery craftsmen have made use of their diversified talents and methods to remove impurities from molten gold, beat it into sheets, mould it into various shapes by soldering numerous little components of the jewellery and embellish the finished products of their innovative artistic ideas. According to literary sources, Greek craftsmanship had a primary influence in India during the post-Alexander period when Indian gold jewellery craftsmanship grew in imagination in designing, engraving, putting studded gems into the gold and crafting gold jewellery by adopting different culture-specific, religious-specific and belief-specific symbols on the gold jewellery. Hence, the gold craftsmen are meticulously crafting the gold metal to jewellery over the years and have continued to dedicate themselves to specialising in jewellery-making methods and techniques. Even though the norms of the Indian society have changed over the millennium, the knowledge of the Indian gems and jewellery industry is established as an all-inclusive knowledge of innovative ideas connected with gold.

Gold as a commodity develops societal and individual value universally. It was also used for the medium of exchange (gold coins). Gold jewellery first functions the need to fulfil religious and socio-cultural values, and then it appears as a commodity in a form of representation of money, a proof of wealth and power. The opening of market and

DOI: 10.4324/9781032717951-3

unleashing of capitalism in this industry has undoubtedly accelerated the growth of this gold smithery where gold craftsmen began to control the production process to sell their product on the open market. A process of primitive accumulation played its role as gold craftsmen neither identified themselves as capitalist producers nor as workers. This ongoing accumulation of capital increases with a rise of basic consumer tendency to enhance their appearance, attractiveness and prominence by purchasing gold jewellery. The process of making gold ornaments evolved over time into a specialised occupation, which in turn became a hereditary caste occupation,[1] as women, men and children adorned their bodies with gold jewellery (Ketkar, 1990). This propelled the formation of a massive gold jewellery industry.

In exploring the economic sub-system of the hereditary occupations, the matter is made more intricate by the fact that the family as a sub-system has no significant hereditary functional relationship with their caste occupation, as many craftsmen from the other castes (other than *swarnakars*) had trained themselves in manufacturing jewelleries (Glyn & Sutcliffe, 1972, p. 10). This is because they were unable to compete with the industrial goods (produced in England and marketed in Indian market) promoted and developed by the colonial authorities (Mukherjee, 1958; Singer & Cohn, 2001; Desai, 1948). As a result, it caused de-industrialisation in India where the small-scale household manufacturing industries eventually learned to make gold jewellery as it gave them an opportunity to redefine themselves in the jewellery industry (Majumdar et al., 1990, Majumdar, 2004). This shift had happened because of the mounting demand of gold jewellery industry. Due to this fact, many artisanal/ non-artisanal castes had identified themselves as 'gold-makers'. For instance, Bailey discovered that a family of sweepers used to manufacture and repair gold jewellery in Khondmal, Orissa. Over the years the profession of making gold ornaments spread among many Indian castes. In general, there are four categories of *swarnakars*: *kshyatrisonar*, or those who think they are a *kshatriya* sub-caste descended from *suryavanshi*; *ayodhyawasi* or *purabiya sonar*; *mairhkshaytriya sonar*; and *mahawar* or *marwari sonar*.

The social order of the Indian jewellers is recognised by their hereditary occupation instead of their prescribed caste-based occupation. The caste-based social order 'not only prescribes ... a hereditary occupation but also discourages his attempts to surmount the occupational barriers' (Driver, 1962). Flexibility in picking out and accepting a fresh mode of life after involving themselves into this occupation is observed since the 16th century, when many castes have accepted different caste occupations by excluding their prescribed caste occupations (Ghurye, 1950: 15–17). Agriculture, for instance, is common as an occupation for every caste group. This flexibility in choosing caste occupation is not a recent phenomenon; rather it is an effect of British capitalistic rule over India that has dissolved the caste system in terms of economic activity. To some extent, caste continued to play its role in the cultural life of the people in this century, i.e., in the case of marriage (endogamy). It is observed that individuals from different caste backgrounds had accepted goldsmithy as their family occupations. They were successful in upholding and carrying on the family trade of goldsmithy, which finally became their hereditary employment.

Since then, the export of gold jewellery has grown to be one of the major industries in India, which in turn led to an increased demand for Indian-styled jewellery within and outside of the Indian subcontinent.

I carried out the fieldwork from July 2015 to August 2018. I used purposive sampling to gather data from 102 traditional jewellers (including the jewellery shop owners and *karigars*). The qualitative data was gathered through jewellers' case studies. In my fieldwork, I have examined the business strategies (advertisement, offers, networking, exploration of the cultural symbols and strategies to sustain the buying mood by harping on the 'fetish' side of the commodity, playing with the purity game and so on) and the marketing strategies to understand the unrealistic symbols that have created an impact on the consumer and the competitions in the same trade. I interviewed them with the help of an interview schedule for collecting both qualitative and quantitative data about their business, marketing strategies, advertisements, promotional offers, the treatment of their consumers, the problems they encounter, the way they play the gold purity game, the changing jewellery market and so on.

The Unorganised Structure of Gold Jewellery Industry

The structure of the gold jewellery industry will be discussed under three headings: identifying the conventional jewellers and goldsmiths, the organisational structure of the gold jewellery industry and distributive channels in the gold jewellery sector.

Identifying the Conventional jewellers

People who are actively or indirectly involved in the jewellery industry are acknowledged as conventional jewellers and goldsmiths. They fall into two categories: those who are functionally dependent on their family business (hereditary business) and those who learn the craft of jewellery creation via instruction (non-hereditary business). The role of the people's involvement in the jewellery business is organisationally unstructured as far as the social stratification of the local gold jewellery industry is concerned. After the introduction of structural reforms in 1999, an expansion in the gold jewellery industry has occurred in terms of increasing differentiation in various terms of specialised manufacturing and retailing units. The process of differentiation and specialisation has given a specific identity to the conventional jewellers and goldsmiths in India. The majority of the jewellery business falls under the informal sectors; I have categorised them as:

• Goldsmiths or gold jewellery artisans (*karigar*) – They are popularly referred to as *karigars – the makers of gold jewellery* who are the backbone of every jewellery industry in India. They are the ones who add creative flair to gold by using their talent and creative sensibility. Learning this creative art originates in the family for those who keep their hereditary manufacturing jewellery business alive through socialisation and for those who take this training as a means of livelihood. Although, it is primarily a family run business, research shows that neighbourhood relationships, particularly in rural regions, have a significant influence in attracting other people to this line of work. Even the young generations living in rural–urban fringe are often influenced by neighbourhood sentiments to take up this line of work as a start-up business after receiving training from experienced gold craftsmen. They typically avoid selling high-end jewellery directly as they either work for or under other jewellery workshop owners or jewellers. Sometimes, repairing and little modifications of jewellery brought to them by the customer adds an extra earning for a day. Mostly, they generally work on instructions from the jewellery shop owners who pass on the design placed by the customers. However, the design comes to them as a concept and they work out the details. They work on the specified size and weight of the ornament but work out the micro details all by themselves. Their work is broken down into its smaller parts and then re-constructed using jewellery specialists familiar with on '*time – and motion principles*'.[2] They have a horizontally structured scientific work-line, which allows more versatile work specialisation.

• Small-sized Jewellers (local *swarnakars*) – They are the conventional jewellers who have established their own jewellery store where they create jewellery entirely on their own by following caste-based or hereditary occupation across generations. The nature and dynamics of their work are based on the involvement of the family members for making jewelleries. In Marxian term, they are the petty-bourgeois who are involved in petty commodity production.[3] Their manufacturing units are run primarily by family labour and goldsmiths (whose numbers vary depending on the size of the business).

The manufacturing unit is known as workshop which is located behind the shop of all the small and medium-sized jewellers. They supervise goldsmiths and train them in creating a specific design. They identify themselves as middle-middle class and upper-middle class. They pass down their jewellery business knowledge to their present generation and motivate them to continue their hereditary business.

Medium-sized Jewellers (regional *swarnakars*) – These categories of jewellers have been running the inherited family jewellery business for at least four generations. Their jewellery stores are bigger in magnitude and revenue. In order to better serve their customers, they have transformed their jewellery store into a corporate business structure where they have kept specialist personnel for jewellery sections to look over every element of their business, such as financial accounting, monitoring the sales, supervising etc. The member of the owner-family is present in the store in every situation. They have a larger workforce to manage their business such as at least four to six salespeople to handle the customers and a separate jewellery workshop with more than eight goldsmiths or jewellery artisans. The current generation of these entrepreneurial families have access to the knowledge about Indian gems and jewellery industry that has been passed down from earlier generations. Some of the young generations have received academic and official training in management that has helped them to achieve their jewellery business goals in digital age. They are acquainted with governmental actions related to gold and industrial policies, emerging technologies, gold market rates, international competitors/branded jewellery showrooms, consumer expectations, jewellery trends, etc. However, they run their stores by hiring managers having good academic record in business and management so that they can interact with the customers in a professional way. They are the ones that started their chain of businesses by expanding in local and national markets. Therefore, the growth of the jewellery business depends on the mastery over trading knowledge and the skills of the 'manufacturer'. Conventional jewellers, especially small-sized jewellers and goldsmiths, still hold a significant part of the jewellery business in the local or regional market, but they are not interested in expanding their jewellery business regionally or nationally because they lack financial support. Middle-sized jewellers are relatively ambitious and quite capable of becoming a part of a regional brand by expanding their family jewellery business as they have resources to expand their business by opening a chain of shops in different locations by modernising their business management. They try to hold on to the local tradition and culture in order to hold on to their fixed customers.

Organisational Structure of Gold Jewellery Industry

The business structure[4] of the jewellery industry is linked to the economic structure of the gold jewellers as well as the principles of market economy. Marx's theory of class explains the 'plurality of classes'[5] where the middle class works as the lesion between the owning classes and the working classes. Likewise, in the jewellery industry, there are different kinds of owners, managers and workers, who are placed in a hierarchical order, yet united in an overall structure, conflicting and cooperating at times. In the jewellery trade in India, the categories of people involved in a kind of 'class relation' are the goldsmiths/gold artisans (small manufacturer and big manufacturer/middlemen/proletariat), small-sized jewellers (retailing and manufacturing/retailing/wholesalers/petty-bourgeoisie) and middle-sized jewellers (who oversee the jewellery shop/bourgeoisie[6]). The gold jewellery industry is comprised of all these categories of conventional jewellers who are involved in various production process and have established networks based on the nature of their business and working relationships. The relations of production between goldsmiths-small-sized jewellers, goldsmiths-middle-sized jewellers, goldsmiths-managers, managers-middle-sized jewellers, middle-sized jewellers-salesmen and salesmen-small-sized jewellers can be explicated with the help of the following diagram. At the same time, consumers in India play a crucial part in maintaining the organisation of the jewellery industry.

A clear relationship between a manufacturing unit and a wholesaling unit, a wholesaling unit and a retailing unit, a manufacturing unit and a retailing unit and a manufacturing unit cum wholesaling retailing units is shown in Figure 3.1, which shows the structure of the Indian gold jewellery industry. These free-standing units are designed to hold the conventional jewellers – goldsmiths, small and medium-sized jewellers – together into a single cycle so that they can sustain their respective jewellery stores through mutually beneficial

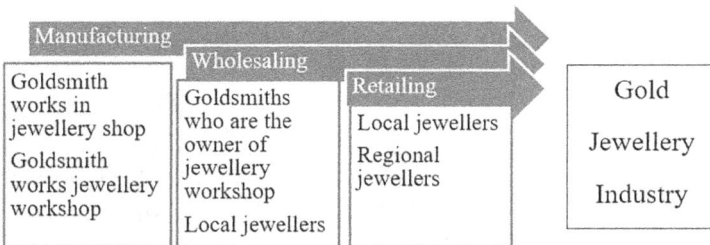

Figure 3.1 Structure of the gold jewellery industry.

trade. They are interconnected structurally in a way that keeps the Indian gold jewellery business viable over time.

A Network: Distributive Channels in the Gold Jewellery Sector

Local jewellery businesses are connected through horizontal (competition within the same group of sectors) and vertical (distributive channel of interdependency) workforces where an economic local network is generated through extensive entrepreneurship. These two aspects relate to the services that suppliers provide and consumers receive, along with the technical equipment needed to make jewellery. The role play of the conventional jewellers in the gold jewellery sector are determined by the type and share of work they do, such as working in small workshops under owner, working with under the small/large workshops or with middle-sized jewellers. It is found that the interdependency and integrated nature of this sectoral network prevails everywhere in this industry and corporate jewellery industries. The nature of the conventional jewellery business is strongly influenced by the distribution route via which gold jewellery is transmitted from manufacturing facilities into the hands of consumers. A conduit, illustrated in figure 3.2, connects the producer and the customer through the intermediaries, establishing a network comprising seven distributive channels within the business structure.

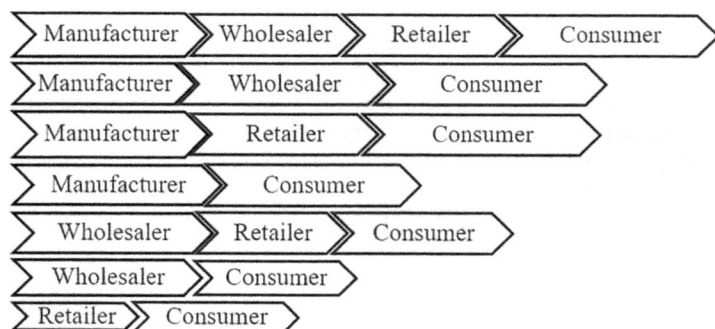

Figure 3.2 Business chain in India.

The amount of gold traded in the jewellery industry is constantly increasing. Numerous jewellery firms have opened storefronts throughout cities as a result of the spike in demand. Gold manufacturing facilities connected to retail stores are the most common type of trade. The largest employers in jewellery trade are the conventional manufacturing and retailing units. The employees of these two units, who are directly or indirectly linked with the consumers, play a significant part in sustaining the hereditary profession. These units recruit workers/employees from diverse economic and educational backgrounds. The current trend in the industry is the growing proportion of organisers, managers, technicians, jewellery designers and administrative staff. In the Indian gold jewellery production industry, there are 55 percent more goldsmiths than employees, and less than 20 percent of the jewellery sectors are organised and operate on a big scale (Pessemier, et al., 2022).

Marketing Structure of the Gold Jewellery Industry

A market is a place for economic activities for individuals and groups to form their economic institutions freely. It is based upon the condition of production, reproduction and consumption of social life where individuals are related and economically dependent on one another. Marx has vividly explained how the production system, along with distribution and consumption constitutes the 'base' or foundation of a social system. The junction between the 'base' and 'superstructure' is the market where an individual involuntarily enters social relations through sale and purchase. Therefore, the concept of market deals with how the producers and sellers are selling their products, how they deal with the demand and supply of the products, how they determine the prices of the products and how they maintain a cordial relationship among the producers, retailers and consumers. The market thrives under neo-liberal policies, where the state grants more and more space to it and amends the credit policy, taxation and labour laws to suit the interests of the market. The market economy thrives by promoting consumerism, i.e., by granting more choice and freedom to the sellers as well as the buyers.

Philip Kotler (et al.) writes: 'Marketing is a societal process by which an individual and groups obtain what they need and want through creating, offering and freely exchanging products and services of values with others' (Kotler, 2013). Sociologically, marketing engages people in exchange of goods and services. In exchange, the jewellers need to know the preferences, needs and tastes of the consumers and the consumers should know about the products the jewellers are out to sell or trade. It works on the principle of reciprocity; there always must be something to offer in exchange from either side. There is a great deal of dynamism in the relationship between the jewellers and consumers. Since the jewellers face competition, they resort to various strategies to outwit others in the business. Jewellers of all sizes try to establish stable relationships with their customers and work on their psyche. A sense of mutual trust and consumer satisfaction comes in handy in building the relationship. For the small and medium-sized jewellers the relationship lasts for generations as the buyers and sellers get into a social relationship. Thus consumers in the middle class may have 'family jewellers' who offer various styles of jewellery for all occasions.

The marketing structure of conventional jewellers was based on meeting local demands. The prime mode of meeting local demand was to build a stable face-to-face interaction with the customers, sometimes by visiting the house of known customers with the design book. Their marketing plans were based on local-regional needs, and their main method of promotion was to develop a steady face-to-face relationship with their intended consumers. The strategy adopted by the jewellery industry, at present, has changed from 'production to consumers' to 'consumers to production' (Bauman, 2007). It signifies that the jewellers have started giving emphasis to the taste of the consumers before making gold jewellery. The industry today creates designs based on their interactions with customers as well as the evolving preferences and wants of customers from various social classes and cultures. These days, the marketing strategy is consumer-focused and evidence-based. The pricing of the gold jewellery is an important component of the marketing plan used by conventional jewellers and traders. As a result, they employ a few covert techniques to increase their profits in the competitive market. But the jewellery sector suffers from a lack of transparency which consumers are unaware of. So, the government has launched and regularised hallmarking of gold jewellery in 2000 to protect the consumer from malpractices of the conventional jewellers. Until 2019, jewellers opposed the move because they thought that the problem would create troubles and hassles and they would not be able to deceive the customers based on the purity of gold.

The Indian jewellery market is highly diversified because of regional variations in consumer tastes and shopping preferences. Mumbai, Chennai, Kolkata and New Delhi are the playing fields of jewellery manufacturing units in India. Other than these cities, Hyderabad, Rajkot, Surat, Jaipur, Coimbatore and other major cities are also developing rapidly (Pessemier et al., 2022). The marketing strategies involve targeting the festive seasons, dates of religious importance, wedding seasons, birthdays, valentine's day and other culturally important days (see Chapter 4). This shows that the 'time of year' plays a very important role in jewellery retailing and market structure where the conventional jewellers mostly in rural India act as a moneylender within their locality. Therefore, the preferred time to sell (sellers' perspective) or purchase (buyers' perspectives) jewellery determine the demand for gold jewellery. Research shows that

32 percent of the consumers preferred to buy jewellery during 'occasions', 20 percent of them prefer to purchase gold jewellery when the 'gold rate is low', 8 percent preferred to buy jewellery when a 'New collection' of jewellery design comes in the market and 8 percent of them preferred to buy jewellery during festivals. Other than these, it is found that 'other' factor includes friends and family members' influence, unexpected gifts to one's loved ones, the downfall of the share market and getting rid of black money, etc. At the same time, gold is consumed in a form of jewellery for its 'eternal quality' (Ertimur & Sandıkcı, 2005, pp. 322–327; Renfrew, 1986) which is a 'store of value for perpetuity' (Menon, 2015: 99–100), arising from the inheritance of jewellery. It is an essential ornament that acts as a bridge to connect individuals, kin members, religious groups and the society.

The marketing strategies that motivate customers to buy jewellery are as follows: wedding, engagement, gift-giving, investment and resale purpose. Research shows that wedding is the main factor that drives customers to purchase jewellery. A new social custom has sprung up around jewellery, such as *exchanging ring* or ring ceremony or engagement, which has become an 'important' ritual in contemporary society. For example: ring ceremony or exchanging rings was mainly the tradition for the non-bengali community but now-a-days it has become a trend even among Bengalis to celebrate ring ceremony.

Research shows that exchanging jewellery in wedding acts as an emotional practice that connects the bride and groom with kin members. It is also believed that the weight and size of the gold jewellery determine the long-term relationship between the receiver and the giver. The practice of giving gold jewellery as a gift symbolically and culturally also connects the receiver and the giver. It has become a compulsion that facilitates one to showcase one's social standing in the family, friends or neighbourhood. So, the marketing strategies and market structure are not always based on economic rationality; rather they acquire legitimacy from inherited jewellery. The jewellery market structure is socially reproduced and constructed by everyday practices related to cultural practices.

Market Competitions in the Same Trade

The factor that creates 'competition' among the corporate branded jewellery houses is unambiguously a socio-economic urge to grow and expand their branded jewellery company in various areas. Their main motive is to make a profit. Max Weber has termed it as an 'exploitation of market situation' (Swedberg, 1999, p. 219) where the marketer tries to get hold of the market by controlling the means of production and services of the employees for ensnaring the consumers. Indian consumers have acknowledged corporate branded jewellery houses as the best-known 'brands'. So, the regional *swarnakars* were forced by the market situation to adopt a rational and strategic approach by modernising their jewellery stores (adapting the infrastructural changes of their jewellery outlets), complying with market regulations, adopting new technology and innovating their business practices. This has increased competition among both branded jewellery companies and regional/local *swarnakars* because the preferential treatment given to certain regional brands has opened up opportunities for regional jewellers to successfully promote their jewellery business and compete with well-established corporate showrooms such as Tanshiq/Senco Gold and Diamond).

Brand Preference is attached to the emotional response of the consumers towards the gold jewellery products. For example, consumers preferred Tanishq because of their offers, jewellery designs, lightweight jewellery, hospitability and mostly for the availability of *karatmeter.*[7] The area of conflict of popular branded corporate jewellery showrooms is defined by the incompatibility of their brands when compared with other brands, situated in the same location. These well-known corporate brands specialise in the manufacturing and marketing of jewellery, establishing their distinct identity as the unparalleled jewellery store-houses that showcase exquisite gold jewellery. Their uniqueness lies in their ability to cater to the discerning tastes of consumers, thus bridging a chasm between jewellery products and consumer preferences for gold jewellery. The exclusivity of these brands, coupled with their areas of conflict, has further widened this gap, while their relationship with traditional jewellers continues to be a significant factor. This has led to covert competition between branded corporate jewellers and conventional jewellers.

Bauman in his article 'The Self in a Consumer Society' has explained how the consumers in the consumer society are differentiated from those in the other types of society. He writes, 'What we do have in mind is that our "consumer society" in the similarly profound and fundamental sense in which the society of our predecessors, modern society in its industrial phase, used to be a "producer society"' (Bauman, 1999, p. 36). He commented that the consumers rule the society. Our neo-liberal society has given opportunities to the consumers to open their own business with a distinct taste in the field in order to meet the consumer desire and fetish for an object (jewellery). It has given an opportunity to every people to be a part of the open market (market situation). However, the market is characterised by an uneven competition among the big traders and the small traders. Every conventional jeweller and jewellery trader (middle-sized jewellers) lags behind the branded corporate jewellers in terms of publicity stratagem.

The popular branded corporate jewellers have been making use of their brand name and have spread the awareness about their jewellery products through social media. This platform of social media has emerged as a core of the present-day society, which is best used by the corporate jewellers to evoke the buying desire and the passion for the modern designs they promote through meticulous research and market survey. They constantly work on strategies for reaching out to the consumers and creating a stable consumer base. They also know the art of continually satisfying their customers with their sophisticated sales strategies. They take recourse to all types of advertisements to promote their brand. They use jewellery advertisements in the form of hoardings, magazines, television commercials and newspaper ads to catch the eye of the readers or passers-by. In this way, the big branded corporate jewellers try to appeal to the psyche of the consumers who end up purchasing jewellery from their branded corporate showrooms.

The conventional jewellers, especially small-sized jewellers and goldsmiths, are unable to afford such means of luring consumers towards their jewellery shop; but middle-sized jewellers do go for advertising their shops and jewellery products in local television channels, local newspapers and sometimes road-side hoardings. Side by side, they also give an opportunity to the consumers to alter their designs, types and style of the jewellery according to their preference, which the branded corporate jewellers are unable to provide to the consumers. The popular brands need at least 20–30 days for altering or repairing as compared to the instant service given by the conventional jewellers. This is the key to the survival of the conventional jewellers for many generations. This shows that there are factors that work in favour of the unorganised conventional jewellers, allowing them space for survival in Indian gold jewellery market. A good businessperson knows the skills for maintaining, retaining and bringing consumers to their shop. Thus, Bauman is right in saying: 'modern society has little need for mass industrial labour and conscript armies, but it needs – and engages – its members in their capacity as consumers' (Bauman, 1999, p. 36). This shows that the apparently competing players in jewellery trade can coexist and find their distinctive spaces of operation. The central thesis is that competition is a process that was established with the market, and that the market and the market process is jointly established with the organisational division of labour (Metcalfe et al., 2003, p. 73). Thus, every jewellery business as an organisation faces different types of competition focusing on production cost, technological knowledge, qualitative norms, policies, customary habits and beliefs, market share, business strategy, marketing strategies and approaches. Max Weber identified these forms of competitions as a 'peaceful conflict' which is forcing the organisations to take some efforts to 'gain control over opportunities and advantages which are also desired by others' (Metcalfe et al., 2003, p. 77). Thus, contemporary cultural industry is a mixture of market approaches, unorganised business sectors and multi-cultural communities with heterogeneity of relationships. These unorganised jewellery industries continue to dominate Indian jewellery manufacturing and retailing sectors.

The Organised Gold Jewellery Industry

For the sale of gold jewellery, the corporate jewellery sector is acknowledged as a well-organised industry. It consists of multinational jewellery enterprises that have entered the territory of conventional jewellers by proving their manufacturing and trading skills. The structure of the gold jewellery market in India has been significantly impacted by the advent of corporate styled jewellery, altering consumer preferences and the practise of rationalisation employed by the corporate jewellery sector. These factors have also changed the country's cultural and economic setting. These big business sectors have McDonaldized (Walter, 2010, pp. 199–201, 223–230) their trade and production as part of their business strategy, by constructing layers of myths or false values that operate in the minds of the potential customers constructing jewellery purchase as a mark of social status and making them compulsive buyers. Their main motive is to reorganise the diversified consumers' preferences under one frame of homogeneity where they will obtain their desired product from the same set of choices given to them. This strategy has four essential facets – efficiency, calculability, predictability and controllability. These facets have levitated the fashion sense of the jewellery among the consumers where the corporate jewellers with their designer manufacturing units try to manufacture gold jewellery at an affordable price by reducing the carat of gold for making trendy gold jewellery. It meets consumer demands for lightweight gold jewellery with weights that have been reduced from 22 carats to 18 carats to 10 carats.

These jewellery houses follow a 'rational' division of labour where the workers are formally recruited based on specialisation with a higher division of responsibilities among different working departments and sections. Here the working relations are maintained through a set of rules and regulations of the trade. Formal education up to the required standard is mandatory. The work organisation is hierarchical in nature, which follows administrative order, with decisions flowing from the top to the bottom and their efficiency is measured in terms of customer's satisfaction. Moreover, their marketing strategies determine the jewellery market-segmentation and targeting, positioning a positive image of brand, marketing four Ps (Product, Price, Place and Promotion), positing customer-relational management, brand and service equity etc. They are identified as corporate branded jewellery houses or showrooms because they are 'characterised by separation of ownership and managements, and the financing of corporations by sales to the public of shares in the possible returns from future operations' (Gerth & Mills, 1946, p. 68).

Organised jewellery sectors are characterised by having a chain of jewellery showrooms in regional, national and multinational levels with a strong brand image which targets largely urban consumers belonging to upper-middle class and above. The organisational structure of the corporate power has influenced indigenous material and non-material culture very effectively. It has made controlling of management relatively easy as they evaluate the tasks based on educational and experiential knowledge. Hence, the result is a bureau-cratisation of administration in which making a profit is a constant economic activity that grows as a result of advertisement and has always been a distinctive development of administrative task. The largest organised jewellery houses in India are Tanishq, Malabar Gold and Diamond, Kalyan Jewellers, P C Jewellers, P C Chandra Jewellers, etc. According to the Managing Director, India of World Gold Council, India's gold industry is becoming more organised as the retailers with larger regional and national chain are gaining market share, having introduced sophisticated inventory management and well-crafted advertising campaigns that meet the demands of young urban consumers. Side by side, the electronic and outdoor media along with Online media (Amazon, Flipkart, Companies' websites, etc.) are playing a major role in jewellery advertisements. The topmost organised jewellery houses invest substantial amounts of money in marketing. Jewelleries spent between Rs 3,400mn and Rs 3700mn (US$ 56mn and US$58mn) on television advertising from 2013–15 (India's gold market: evolution and innovation, 2017, pp. 28–30). It is observed that Titan Company *CaratLane* is dominating in online advertisements by focusing on lightweight jewellery at an affordable price. Currently, it is observed from the research that a vast majority of the conventional jewellers are becoming organised as well. Hence, the main objective of every organised jewellery sector is to revise their business and marketing strategies to hold onto the consumers and jewellery market and to enhance their brand image. They have also started promoting seasonal and local jewellery based on festivals, cultural events and religious dates. This has induced several brands to expand their chain of business in urban areas.

Notes

1 Hereditary and the prescribed occupations became one of the principles of Indian caste system (Bhatt, 1975) and all the castes started being known by their occupational name (Ghurye 1966), like *swarnakars* meaning goldsmiths. Due to this, swarnakars is the common terminology used to identify gold-smiths/jewellery makers/jewellers in India. They held a higher position in the society in comparison with the other artisanal castes.

2 'Taylorist principles of rationalisation through the separation between the planning and the execution of the labour, plus continual mechanism' (Bottomore, 2000, p. 462).

3 'The handicraftsman or peasants who produces with his own means of production will either gradually be transformed into a small capitalist who exploits the labour of others, or he will suffer the loss of his means production ... and be transformed into a wage-labourer. This is the tendency in the form of society in which capitalist mode of production pre-dominates', Gibbon and Neocosmos argues by quoting Marx in Theories of Surplus Value, Vol. 3, (Gibbon & Michael, 1985).

4 It is a 'process who interact with whom and how: between two people who know each other (network) or between two groups in different positions vis-a-vis power (manager versus employees – those who control labor versus those who work). Structure shapes actions by providing resources – people who provide information or other help, right to use money and property, and so on. Structure is the distribution of resources and the power to act' (Hass, 2007, p. 9).

5 Alan Swingehood's (2000) explains that other than two halves of the class struggle; an intermediate class also belongs which he called as middle class.

6 Poulantzas (1975) in his book Classes in Contemporary Capitalism defines bourgeoise in terms of real economic control of means of production and of the product (economic ownership) and the capacity to put the means of production into operations (possession) (Bottomore, 2000, p. 57).

7 Non-invasive method of quality testing of gold jewellery.

4 Indian Culture and Consumption of Gold Jewellery

Indian Jewellery Market and Consumers

A class situation is one in which there is a shared typical probability of procuring goods, gaining a position in life, and finding inner satisfaction.

Max Weber (1978)

Neo-liberalism is founded on the belief in the unrestricted market where consumers can purchase and spend their money based on their free choice. It provides choices to the consumer – the more the demands of the consumers towards the product, the more the supply of products in the market, and these products will escalate the requirement of the market, which will immediately bring profit to the producer. It provides an open space for marketers to establish their businesses by unlocking trade barriers and the consumers with the liberty to pursue their self-interest in buying products. The neo-liberal market has groomed the consumers as their agents who influence the market (Castro, 2015). This neo-liberal market perpetually flourishes by arousing the consumers' uncontrollable passion for material objects or commodities. It gives rise to the passion for buying or keeping the commodities available in the marketplace so that the consumers can draw mystical satisfaction from such acquisition. The Indian jewellery market is evolving towards a consumer-targeted market where it is focusing not only on retaining and sustaining the consumers for the long term but also on retaining and sustaining their business. Over the last few decades, the number of consumers has swelled with the rise in purchasing power of the burgeoning middle – and upper classes. Consumers are the key element for every jewellery house, and for the jewellery market. Gold jewellery in India is not merely for personal adornment but it has an underneath mystic meaning that is connected with sacredness and purity.

DOI: 10.4324/9781032717951-4

The value of gold jewellery, be it a belief or as an artefact, plays a significant role in expanding the cultural heritage of Indian society. The tradition of carrying on the social value of gold jewellery lies in these two major segments – first, as an artefact – the value of gold jewellery has grown stronger over the years for its economic meaning, used as an investment at the time of need; and second as 'belief' – it has been cultural practice for ornamentation and status symbol. It is connected to the way of life, attitude and societal norms of people that continued from one generation to another through socialisation. The religious beliefs associated with metallic gold and gold jewellery is the prime factor for practicing the tradition of buying/gifting gold jewellery whenever an occasion demands it. The continuation of buying gold jewellery is considered when the next generation takes up the tradition of customary rituals linked with gold jewellery. However, the patterned behaviour of people buying gold jewellery in India is undergoing an evolutionary change and this modification is happening in a multi-dimensional mode where a multitude of cultures has created a melting pot of all the beliefs allied with gold jewellery, and as a consequence, the social value of gold jewellery is in transition. As jewellery is seen to be an integral part associated with the body, it has its significant attachment to our daily life which keeps the emotional bond of the wearer, the giver and the one who possesses it.

My fieldwork for this research was conducted from July 2015 to December 2016, and again in 2018. The research involved in-depth interviews with 102 conventional jewellers and 50 consumers using a purposive sampling approach to gather primary data. During the interviews, an interview schedule was used to collect information on their culture and consumption of gold jewellery.

Religious Beliefs, Cultural Practises and Consumption of Gold Jewellery

In India, consumption of gold jewellery is a cultural phenomenon which allows Indian consumers to make their free choice in selecting the jewellery they want to for adornment. It is attached with beliefs and practises emerging as customs. After China, India ranked second in terms of largest gold-consuming country. According to a 2018 report by the National Institution for Transforming India (NITI Aayog), a think tank run by the Indian government, the country's gem and jewellery market is worth approximately Rs. 650,000 crores (94.9 billion dollars), with micro, small and medium-sized businesses contributing to 90–95 percent of national industrial production of gold jewellery. Neo-liberalism has encouraged people to keep up their religious beliefs and cultural practises of purchasing gold because it can be sold or mortgaged at the time of financial need. The establishment of a new production facility for making gold products has taken on new significance as a result of a micro entrepreneur's perception of aesthetic and cultural value of gold jewellery (Nanda, pp. 26–79, 198–199).

Mr G Ganguli, *karigar*, says that there is a long tradition which is continuing in our culture that the father should serve food (annaprasan) to the newborn child to eat from the golden spoon at the time of first rice eating ceremony, or should offer a gift in form of jewellery made up of gold – like gold earring/chain/ring to the child (Nanda, pp. 138–139; Menon, 2015, p. 16). The object gold is needed to perform such sacred ritual in our society but then again few alterations in practising this ritual has been observed in this contemporary society. Firstly, instead of father, any other member of a family can perform the ritual and secondly, it not possible to own a golden spoon because of its high economic value so a silver spoon has taken on its significant role. However, it is still believed that for the betterment of the child, gifting of gold jewellery is an unavoidable ritual as it will protect the child against curses and injuries after wearing the jewellery.

Another respondent, name Mrs S Das, has a different ritual for *annaprasan*. She termed it as *mukhe-bhaat (first rice-eating ceremony)*, where the father of the child will dip a gold ring or any gold object in the food which is going to be served to the child and will make the child touch the gold object with his/her tongue.

This highlights the fact that gold jewellery plays a significant role in Hindu rituals. A change in the custom observed among the lower-income people is that if golden spoon and gifting of gold jewellery are not possible for them, then touching of gold jewellery by the child will bring a stroke of good luck to the child. Mrs. Das also says that wearing gold jewellery will allow people to receive divine power (*shakti*), reduce the negative energy from the body of the wearer and will protect the child from the evil eye.

Mr P Munshi, age 42, says I have seen my grandmother wearing heart-shaped design gold jewellery. She loves and prefers heart-shaped jewellery. At the time of my wedding when she took out her golden bracelet mounted with a heart-shaped design for gifting my wife, I teased her for favouring heart-shaped designs. She then expressed her choice for preferring this shape in gold jewellery as the shape taken from *Paan*/betel leaf. It is not the shape of a heart symbolising love. It is a shape taken from *paan* as it is a sacred element for Hindus. Carrying/keeping *paan* will protect oneself from evil powers. It is a complex task to carry/keep a fresh *paan* with oneself regularly. As gold is a sacred metal, and protects people from unevenness, so the shape of *paan* is metaphorically used for making gold jewellery to protect people from negativity and would be easy to carry/keep sacred *paan* design gold jewellery by adorning it over the body. It is also a symbol of loyalty, love and fertility.

Likewise, Mrs P Raha, age 56, says that paddy is considered auspicious among Hindus so the jewellery design is designed like the symbol of paddy i.e. 'V' in shape.

Thus, we can see the potentiality of the goldsmiths(*karigars*) to implant the design onto the jewellery to continue the faith that was built in the name of divine power. At present, this type of shapes indicates atypical meaning rather than religious beliefs. For example, the shape of *'paan'* depicts the shape of 'heart' which means 'love'. So, these types of symbols in jewellery are still in demand but having different meanings attached to them (OH! MY GOLD [Television Series], 2013). Here, we can see the close association with the design of gold jewellery and religious rituals/belief and it is regenerating the social value of gold jewellery in this contemporary society with their hidden meaning. We can easily find that there is a continuity in jewellery designs but a change is observed in terms of the meanings attached to it.

Mr U Prashad, *karigar*, also has faith in religious symbols that are implanted in jewellery design. He says, gold is a divine metal and if any religious symbol is made of divine metal then it will bring positivity in the life of the wearer.

From olden times to the present-day, gold jewellery plays an integral part in religious ceremonies. It has been observed that the Hindu calendar (*panjika, panchangam*) plays an imperative role in the life of the Hindus where certain dates are assigned as an auspicious time for purchasing gold jewellery.

Mr S Talukdar, being a Bengali, expresses her view on the importance of Bengali calendar *'panjika'* which identifies a good time to buy new gold coin/gold jewellery. For her family, an auspicious day to purchase gold jewellery starts with Bengali New Year i.e. during *Akshaya Tithiya (month of April/ VaishakShikla-paksha)*. On this day she worships Lord *Vishnu* as *Lakshminarayan* at a specific time/*puja muhurat* assigned in *panjika. In Hindi belt of India, Akshaya Tithiya is popularly known as Akha Teej. It is a sacred day for Hindus and Jain communities.* It is believed that purchasing gold on this day will bring good luck and success to the family.

Similarly, there are a few more festive occasions to buy gold jewellery, like *Diwali/Dhanterus, Onam, Daserra* and *Pongal*. Other than these festivals, gold jewellery is also purchased at the time of birthday, first rice-eating ceremony of a newborn child, anniversary, wedding seasons etc. Hindu wedding season is also mentioned in Hindu Calendar and it depends on astrology and Planetary change of horoscope. Considering the socio-economic life of the Indians, they were mostly engaged in primary occupations. During those times of the year when the returns of the hard work were received, they preferred spending at the wedding which is associated with giving gifts. Analytically, this procedure indicates that the harvest season gives good fortune to the family, which is connected to an influx of wealth into the family, creating a chance for the marriage to take place. In our civilisation, it has been customary to adhere to the same culture, customs (and seasons) over time because gold is a crucial component of marriage. According to Vedic astrology, God *Brihaspati* is the name of Jupiter, whose body is covered with gold and who brings good luck to the wearer of gold jewellery.

One of the astrologers (name not mentioned), spoke about some beliefs associated with metal gold – firstly, buying gold jewellery at prescribed time is mentioned in Bengali/Hindi calendar as bringing fortune to the family. Secondly, wearing a piece of gold jewellery will invite positive energy to the body and contribute to good health. The astrological stone tied with gold signifies a hidden meaning that safeguards the wearer. For example – a ring in the middle finger will bring fame, in the index finger for increasing concentration, ring finger for strong marital bond and little finger for health issues, and thirdly, the astrological stone will swiftly function if it is covered with gold. He added that another belief related with gold is that wearing *mangalsutra* or gold pendent around the neck in a form of chain or necklace will help the couple from marital problems.

This clearly shows that various interpretations have been constructed in order to comprehend the intimate relationship between the usage of gold jewellery and the Hindu religion. Entrepreneurs who are not in the jewellery industry also wait for these favourable dates to open up a new store, start new companies or even begin with auditing. This illustrates how sensitive Indian civilisation and culture are about giving and receiving gold jewellery as per the calendar. However, in today's world, Indian consumers who live in macro-entrepreneurial areas have less faith in religious beliefs; but they still adhere to traditions and practices such as buying gold jewellery according to calendar dates. For them, it is a day for receiving gifts, purchasing gifts for others or strengthening one's own financial situation (Bauman, 2007, p. 11) because entrepreneurs promote their brands, offer different forms of jewellery and provide discounts on gold jewellery during those times. Contrarily, consumers in the so-called micro-native entrepreneurial areas have a traditional tendency of believing that purchasing gold jewellery will bring luck to life and the family. Regardless of religious-cultural beliefs, the practice of purchasing gold jewellery according to the calendar is still a habit in digital

India. The consumer (pre-dominantly the middle class) not only believes in astrology and theology to follow the Hindu calendar while consuming gold jewellery but via social realities produced by the jewellery entrepreneurs on continuing their theological belief to promote and sell jewellery (Bourdieu 1999:53). Here, consumer's personal behaviours and stimulation from the environment created by the people might generate common social behaviour which signifies that those members of a class share a common lifestyle (Weber, 1978). For these reasons, consuming gold jewellery on those auspicious days has become a part of religion.

Adorning with jewellery is closely connected with women and men in Muslim Society. But among men there is some controversy in this present era since they do not prefer to adorn themselves with jewellery. The usage of gold among them is for personal beautification for women and mosque decoration (Atei et al., 2015). Muslim women prefer to wear Islamic-designed jewellery and minakari jewelleries. Unlike Hinduism, Muslim culture does not have a strong relationship between gold jewellery and religion. Hence buying jewelleries has nothing to do with their religious faith. For them, gift-giving is a customary practice which is encouraged culturally and religiously; as it implies a gesture to spread the love for the family and friends. It is the customary rituals practiced in the name of Prophet Muhammad, who recommended his followers to abide by this cultural practice in the name of 'Allah'. They perform it as a customary practise and ritual at the time of *Eid-Al-Fitr* and end day of *Ramadan.* They gift clothes, perfume, food and other material objects, including jewelleries. Gift-giving in this era has become a shared practice among the people, so in order to mould and establish a new habit among Muslims of buying jewellery throughout the festive season, corporate jewellery shops have started to advertise their jewellery even during Muslim festivals. This is especially true on these two occasions. Corporate jewellers have created particular urges through promotional offers and commercials to affect their psychology by trying to persuade them to buy gold jewellery, gold pendants and gold coins as gift-giving traditions. It is an adaptive process that aids in preserving their sense of community.

One of the respondents named Mrs K. Khatun, age 48, says that even though she is a Muslim, she buys gold jewellery during *Poila Baishak* and *Akshaya Trithiya* because she believes that if "good luck" befalls the family after buying it on a particular day and time, then it is worthwhile to acquire gold jewellery during the Hindu festive period.

A sales representative from corporate jewellers, Mr Choudhury said, we try to promote Muslim design jewellery during *Eid-Al-Fitr* and *Ramadan.* We make calls to registered customers at no cost to them and pass messages on their festivals to make them aware of new gift-giving jewellery collection available at our showroom. Their choice of jewellery is religiously specific so they keep gold pendant, lockets, gold coins with Islamic symbol inscribed on them.

To create a purchasing habit of the Muslim community, macro entrepreneurs (corporate jewellers) are trying to take advantage of the sentiments by redirecting them to favour gold jewellery for giving a gift during their festivals. This attempt of constructing a new attitude among Muslims succeeded when Muslims started communicating with the corporate jewellers for gift-giving on their religious occasions. This cultural force has influenced the traditional role-structure of Muslim community where economically downgraded people are preferring to visit MSMEs *(traditional jewellers and artisans)* during their festivals for buying jewellery.

According to another sales representative from corporate jewellers, Mr. Majumdar, the success of their jewellery shops depends on different types of customers, so they stock jewellery for diverse kinds of communities. For examples, they keep Lord Buddha pendant for Buddhists, for Muslims they keep Ear rings (*Jumkhas, Balis, Pasa*) and gold coin and gold biscuits inscribed 'Allah' in the Urdu Language, Nepali Jewellery, South Indian temple jewelleries, North Indian jewelleries and jewellery mounted with original gemstone or artificial gemstone.

According to the Buddhist and Jain texts, the gold industry flourished during the later Vedic period. The glory of adorning gold jewellery over the body had started from this period but wearing gold jewellery did not have any significant role in Buddhism *per se*. The religious teaching of *Dhamma* portrays that the monks and nuns are not permitted to wear any forms of jewellery during the time of retreat or at the time of meditation because to achieve salvation in life, one should give up all pleasures of modern life and material objects. They symbolise gold with fire and sun, which is attributed to good knowledge, sacredness, bliss, enlightenment and liberty. For making gold jewellery, gold is mixed with other metals such as copper, bronze or silver, which pollutes the purity of gold. Due to this, gold is used in the form of art in Buddhism but not in the form of gold jewellery. Except for monks and nuns, the devotees make gold jewellery in the form of a pendant. These pendants have some specific symbolic religious designs which are tied/painted with gold; such symbols are: pairs of Gold Fish symbolising overcoming of difficulties, Gold Lotus Fish symbolising the attainment of the cleanliness of body, verbal communication, saving mind from negativity and Gold Dharma Chakra symbolising avoiding indulgences (Gold in Buddhism, 2017). During the reign of Lord Buddha, all sections of people who are hierarchically segregated and placed based on their caste structure, possess the previously mentioned four symbols in gold jewellery. Only the rich class of people and kings consumed gold jewellery for personal adornment and for decorating animals, such as elephants and horses. For these reasons, both the micro jewellers and corporate jewellers sell pendants that depict the whole sitting posture of Buddha's body on Buddha Purnima. The social value of gold jewellery is not directly proportional to religious belief, rather it is the producer who is trying this method to induce consumers to purchase jewellery during the festive season.

In this era, 'the society of producers' (term used by Bauman), be it corporate jewellers or micro-native jewellers, are playing an important role in preserving the religious belief by routinizing the behaviour of people to continue their belief on religion – be it a symbolic meaning for Hindus or 'gift-giving' for Muslims or for 'happiness' or other communities. They are trying to maintain cultural solidarity by providing common offers for each religious occasion. A festival is an event that brings all ethnic groups together where the buying behaviours are religiously specific but not religiously bound. The overarching goal of all jewellers is to give the impression that their customers' requests will be met, even if there are already predefined requirements that apply to all customers. Instead, the customer is given the impression that everything is tailored to her needs and wants. The consumers thereby become the 'object of cultural industry' (Adorno & Horkeimer, 1972, pp. 141, 142).

As a matter of fact, gold jewellery in contemporary India has a symbolic connotation where the cultural practices and social value attached to gold jewellery do not play any deciding role in preserving the religious beliefs associated with 'sacredness' of gold jewellery; rather rationality for purchasing gold as a status symbol, prestige and liquidity is the prime objective of Indian consumers. It is the myth which the micro jewellers and the advertising agencies of Corporate Brands try to connect to the tradition by giving a reason for buying gold jewellery at *Dhanterus* and *Akshaya Trithiya* in the form of modern individual choice (Barthes, 2009). It is a practice disseminated by them for its use value and exchange value.

Rationality, Culture and Consumption of Gold Jewellery

Gold jewellery has always been a source of social and financial strength. For ages, people have tried to acquire this precious metal to be exchanged for its monetary value. India has experienced various invasions by various rulers but what did not change over the years is the value of gold as it is associated with the economic and political development of society. Even the Zamindars used to show their supremacy and powers with the amount of gold they possessed.

Gold in the form of coins and bars has always tempted people to purchase and keep it for future security. Eventually, in this era, purchasing/giving gold jewellery is rationally valued more when it is measured by its monetary value rather than its religious value, i.e., 'sacredness'.

Mrs S R Chowdhury (age 40), Mrs S Das (age 55), Mrs S Chatterjee (age 50), Mrs G Sarkar and many other respondents have accepted the social value attached with gold jewellery at the time of the wedding. The common view is that the father of the bride buys gold jewellery at the time of *Diwali* or *Dhanterus* or *Akhshaya Tithiya* during the festive season; for gifting the daughter at the time of her wedding. It is a rational practise to plan for the future in a systematic way to invest money in gold jewelleries on religiously prescribed dates/times as the jewellers offer to provide discounts, offers, exchange of old jewelleries with the new one, etc., which minimizes the financial burden for the wedding. Thus, gold jewellery serves as an investment for the father of the bride. It is uncommon in Indian society for a bride to get more gold jewellery from the groom's side, and if she receives then this is a sign of love and acceptance from groom's family.

The interpretation of Mr. P. Nandi, a 45-year-old man, is another rational justification for owning gold jewellery. He reveals that six years before demonetization, his wife had bought him a gold chain. During the time of demonetization, he was unable to obtain money from the bank due to long queues, nor could he use an ATM. He then mortgaged his gold chain to the conventional jeweller in his family. He proudly proclaimed that the sum he received was far greater than the cost price and also mentioned how high the gold market was at the time of a mortgage. This demonstrates that social security still places a high value on gold.

For these reasons, gold jewellery is still considered as the best investment for future security as the value of gold increases over time. It can always be utilised to get liquidity at the time of need by keeping it as a mortgage, selling it to the jewellers and to get a loan at a time of need. Although it is not used as currency, it is always considered powerful as a store of value. People used to store gold jewelleries because the value of gold was never supposed to go down, and the same can be passed on from generations to generations to maintain the social security.

To quote Menon, 'In modern times, interest has grown in gold as purely an investment medium, the market has begun demanding gold nearly-fine quality ... a purity of 99.99 percent, as close to pure 24-carat gold as is practically possible' (Menon, 2015, p. 121). We can see that the advertisers bring all the means to sell gold jewellery to the consumers. Sometimes they advertise it as investment by spreading the awareness of

Hallmark Jewellery (22 carat). They also advertise lightweight jewellery at a cheaper rate with 10 carats to 18 carat gold jewellery. It is mystifying the consumers by reducing the quality of gold jewellery into 10 carat jewellery as the price of the gold jewellery will be comparatively low which will enable the consumer to purchase it. On the contrary, it is found that the young consumers favoured the fineness of gold to be 22 carats because the universally accepted carat, which is signed as Pure, is the 22 carat. It is the highest carat, by which Indians universally make their gold jewellery. Exceptions prevail in case of Nepali gold and South Indian temple jewelleries (24 carats).

Ms R Subba and Ms N Rai have stated that buying gold for marriage purpose or to gift to their kin, they make gold jewellery made up of 24 carats. Their types of gold jewellery are known as Nepali Gold Jewellery where the gold jewellery is made up of specific traditional designs. Even if they had to wear gold jewellery for daily wear purpose, they prefer 24 carat gold jewellery. They neither compromise on the gold purity nor do they try to deviate from their culture of reducing the purity of the gold from 24 to 22 carat.

The gold market applies a constant market policy to drive the consumer to go for 22 carats. This has generated a habit among consumers to mentally adapt purity to be as 22 carat. Despite this, the Nepali consumers are strongly attached to 24 carat when they purchase gold jewellery.

Prior to 2000, KDM[1] (jewellery with cadmium solder) was used to determine the purity of gold, making it impossible for consumers to determine the exact level of purity. The reasons for purchasing gold jewellery for personal use, a wedding, a dowry or financial security are still valid today as investment. However, today society is providing new certification on the purchase of every gold item that has led to a strong incentive to the consumers to purchase Bureau of Indian Standard Hallmarked gold jewellery. This is because the interest earned by consumers on keeping their money in savings banks keeps on fluctuating, but the value of gold has increased exponentially during the last 60 years. This has stimulated common people to invest in gold as a result of changes in governmental policies and the nation's economic situation (Gold Rate Historical data for India, n.d.).

Mrs. P. Sharma, a 35-year-old, expressed her opinion that people who couldn't afford gold jewellery would trade in their old pieces KDM jewellery or gold coins to get certified Hallmarked jewellery from a legitimate seller or sell their old gold jewellery and make the most money possible. In her view, old KDM gold jewellery or gold coins can be an investment if chosen correctly. She recommended staying away from trading gold jewellery for diamonds or artificial stones as the market value of these stones will never replace the value of gold jewellery.

Likewise, a similar concept has evolved with an easier transaction for the consumers in forms of schemes and bonds. All the interviewees agreed that buying gold is 'a good investment', but it does not mean that they buy gold 'only for investment'. In times of social unrest brought on by the economy, purchasing gold jewellery remains a rational invest-ment. It has historically served as financial support and continues to do so today.

The Indian government has introduced two methods for purchasing gold. First, a method for purchasing the material gold is in the form of jewellery, bars or coins. Currently, gold prices are at an all-time high, making it hard even for middle-class people to buy gold jewellery. The corporate jewellery showrooms have introduced a new programme called Gold Saving Scheme (Monthly Scheme for 12 months or 6 months), that allows buyers to acquire gold jewellery by paying a certain amount of cash on a monthly or weekly basis to the respective jewellery shop as per the scheme. Traditionally it was known as '*khata* system', where the consumers used to pay the amount of gold jewellery to the conventional jewellers on instalment-basis where they can pay a flexible amount to the *swarnakar* at whatever time/day they choose. The corporate jewellers have used a similar strategy to target the middle class by creating a paper contract that looks like an agreement between the business and the customer to make payment on a specific day of each month. On the final day of the agreement, the customer can purchase gold jewellery with that stored amount.

Mr D Mazumdar, says 'At the end of the term of the Gold Scheme, consumers can purchase gold jewellery at the value equivalent to the deposit money adding some interest by the respective jewellery shop/showrooms. These forms of strategies have introduced easy accessibility in purchasing gold jewellery without mental/economic burden for those individuals who belong to the middle class and the lower-class groups'.

The second method for investment in gold is materialised in the form of documentation, which is known as 'paper gold'. In this, people purchase Gold Bonds and Gold Exchange Traded Funds (ETF) (Dhawan, 2019), which provide interest to people, like physical gold. Trading in gold also provides an alternative direction for the investors to invest in raw gold. As a paper asset based on gold, it also continued to be the first choice of investment for the young citizens who considered that this method of investment will save them from paying an additional amount, such as gold jewellery making charges, storage and packaging costs, GST and so on. The main objective of 'paper gold' is to get the market value of gold in the future. The eight largest gold ETFs are:

- Aditya Birla Sun Life Gold Fund
- SBI Gold Fund

• Reliance Gold Saving Fund
• Kotak Gold Fund
• ICICI Prudential Regular Gold Saving Fund
• HDFC Gold Fund
• Axis Gold Fund
• Canara Robeco Gold Savings Fund

All these schemes of gold have helped the investors to opt for easy access directly by themselves (Menon, 2015, p. 127). Gold bond is for those consumers who are self-employed, have the least interest in purchasing gold jewellery or are economically independent and/or are not very keen to accumulate gold jewellery in a bigger quantity. It is an easier transaction for the consumers when the banks have started giving gold bonds to the real-time value of gold, which can be purchased and sold at the convenience of the consumers. Since it seems more secured than any other risky investment like lands and shares, people find it more lucrative to invest in gold. In India, purchasing gold jewellery is the core reason for investment. Therefore, India is popularly known as world's largest gold consumer country, holding the 11th largest gold reserves in 2019, where gold was measured to be 607 tonnes, as reported by the World Gold Council. Although the market and price of gold is always unpredictable, it has never shown any drop in price, which may generate loss to the person who possesses gold. It has never crossed its yardstick for the last 60 years. For this reason, the production cost of gold is best for investment rather than investment in diamond jewellery (Bose, 2013). Eventually, in this contemporary India, giving gold jewellery is valued more, as it is measured by its monetary value rather than its religious value.

Social Status, Social Bond and Consumption of Gold Jewellery

Max Weber has defined the status situation as, 'every typical component of the life of men that is determined by specific, positive and negative, social estimation of honour' (Gerth & Mills, 1946, p. 187). To him, status is linked with a specific lifestyle, which is immediately connected with the consumption of goods. It will lead people to feel free to take a new identity in the status hierarchy. Consumption of gold jewellery lies in religious practices, whereas wearing it over the body is a socio-cultural practice. It is observed that even the social status of the metal workers, 'during the past two thousand years' were also vertically segregated in terms of caste. For example, Lohar caste holds the third position in caste hierarchy but Sonar caste of Punjab is 'considered as semi-clean by Brahmins', as they were permitted to put on a sacred thread by holding caste status as Vaishya (Mills et al.,

2003, p. 398). This brings out the strict cultural segregation, where the social position was maintained based on the metal in the Indian caste system. As an imaginary rule, the upper caste was allowed to wear jewellery made up of gold and gems, but the lower caste (especially the Sudras)/tribe was not permitted to wear jewellery made with golden metal. They used silver, bronze, copper and other sorts of metal for jewellery (Dube, 2004). Thus, the purity of gold represents a symbol of social status only for higher castes. As mentioned earlier, the use of gold is closely connected with Hinduism, thus the jewellery market is constructed based on religious belief to merchandise gold/gold jewellery. The inclination of people to preserve gold jewellery becomes a habit, rationalised by passing from one generation to another, where the social status of a person depends on the specific honour connected with 'class situation', which is determined by a specific 'style of life' they belonged to.

Equally, we have shown that gold has enjoyed a high position during the ancient and medieval times, where rulers used gold in clothes, utensils, gifting and adornment. In the case of gold jewellery, having a significant collection of fine gold jewellery is sometimes seen as a symbol of financial success and social standing, denoting that a person belongs to a higher class in society. This is so because gold jewellery frequently costs a lot of money. The tradition of holding quantity and quality of one's collections of gold is often perceived as a status symbol that separated one caste from another and one class from another. Those who succeed in keeping gold jewellery embrace power. It is the power to draw the attention of others (who possess less gold jewellery or jewellery made of other metal than gold) to themselves by showing their capability and capacity in preserving gold jewellery, indicating the higher status in society.

According to author Asa Berger, 'the objects and artefacts that play such an important role in our everyday lives ... the importance of material goods to people as giving them a sense of their value and goodness' (Berger, 2014, p. 97), is a part of a habitual exchange of material to build a kinship bond. In Indian society, jewellery made up of gold is held in the form of movable property received by women after the marriage. It is a route whereby a daughter receives gold jewellery from her father, mother, brother and husband at the time of the marriage (or before/after marriage) popularly recognised as *streedhan* (Jolly, 1889, p. 54) coupled with 'dowry'. As a *streedhan*, it is an economic right to accept gold jewellery in the form of a gift (Viswanatha, 1928, p. 225) to secure their future.

Mr B Goswami, age 71, consumer, says that marriage and gold jewellery holds a strong connection as they are inextricably linked with each other. A common proverb goes, 'No gold jewellery means no marriage', which implies that marriage is incomplete without gold jewellery. In the past, the gold jewellery that a woman receives from her parents or while getting married is a traditional example of material possession held by women. But presently, although women may now afford their own jewellery since they are monetarily independent, still wearing gold jewellery is mandatory as it reflects social status of a person.

This illustration means it is the only object that plays a dual role in the life of women – first, it will enhance her beauty after adorning it, and second, she will feel secured for its monetary value, which later on will enhance her social standing in her affinal family. It is a nature of conspicuous consumption where exhibiting gold jewellery by wearing it is not only to showcase beauty but also to represent that the family status can be afforded (Veblen, 2005). Besides, it exposes an intimate connection between gold jewellery and the social status of a person, where gold is used as a token at the time of marriage for showcasing family prestige to heighten their social status in front of the invitees – kin members and community members.

On the other side, the material possession of gold jewellery by the bride will secure her position in the affinal family. More specifically, she will get respect, honour and love from affinal kin members. This means that the status hierarchy of a person is depending on the amount of gold jewellery she holds. It is seen as a luxury good indicating the status symbol of the wearer.

Mrs M D Dutta, age 31, consumer, says that at the time of *bodhuboron* – the customary ritual performed by my *sasuri*/mother-in-law to receive me after the marriage at their house, she addressed me by saying *lokkhi elo ghore*/Goddess Lakshmi entered her house.

Mrs B Paswan, age 38, consumer, says *Vadhu-griha-pravesh* is a wedding ritual to welcome *ghar ki Lakshmi* when the bride enters grooms house for the first time.

These ritualistic practices are indicating that the new bride will bring good luck, happiness and prosperity to the groom's family. In contemporary society, people perform this ritual only for the sake of saying that the goddess Lakshmi had entered the house with the new bride or that the new bride represents the goddess Lakshmi. The fundamental meaning behind this belief is that she has brought an enormous quantity of gold and money (dowry) with her which will add financial security to the in-law's family. This is a habitual tendency followed by the people in the name of ritual and customs to inherit gold jewellery to unveil family prestige.

Marriage or any social functions are a platform for women to expose their status by showing varieties of gold jewellery after wearing it in various parts of the body. According to Gidden 'adornment is altruistic', which means the wearer of gold jewellery will enjoy wearing it only when the feeling of self-importance is correspondingly reflected from the viewer towards the wearer (Frisby & Featherstone, 1997, p. 207). This is the reason for those who try to fit into the social gathering for fulfilling their desire and to get appreciation from the others. By reaching out for happiness, she tries to please others. They try to please others by giving compliments on jewellery worn by others and expect to get the same compliments from others. This expectation of being recognised is the sole purpose of being admired by others (Frisby & Featherstone, 1997, pp. 206, 207).

Jewellery is valued as a commodity when it is used as an object in ceremonial exchange. The subjective value of the gold jewellery expresses the individual value attached to the gold jewellery. When gold jewellery relates to an individual value, a strong relationship develops between the giver and the receiver of the gold jewellery. In this manner, gold jewellery works as a system of social communication between people. However, in contemporary society, the concept of *streedhan* is not associated with dowry; it means that a woman receives gifts at the time of her marriage. Wearing gold jewellery in Indian culture is a conspicuous consumption (Veblen, 2005) where the main attraction of any social event lies in the jewellery worn by the bride/child/or any female person rather than men wearing gold jewellery. If in case men wear a piece of gold jewellery at the wedding, it will be indicative of a dowry demand at the time of marriage. However, this perception about gold and gold jewellery is a transaction where the contemporary man purchases gold jewellery for showcasing his class (Barthes, 2009).

Likewise, gold jewellery acts as a mediator between the giver and the receiver after it is received at the time of the birth of a child, during the rice-eating ceremony, marriage anniversary, engagements, birthdays and such similar events. It is the sign-in form of gift that publicises commitment to one another. It is deeply attached to emotional assistance. In Indian customs, inherited gold jewellery is given more value than newly purchased ones. There is social, emotional and heritage value associated with gold jewellery, which is passed on for many generations. There is a special sentiment associated with a mother handing over the gold jewellery to daughter-in-law to granddaughter (see Figure 4.1) or mother handing over her inherited jewellery to the daughter/granddaughter (see Figure 4.2).

Gold jewellery is the symbolic representation of a family tradition which provides a sense of being worthy of receiving the jewellery and acceptance of a new member to the family. Mrs S Raha, age 51, another respondent, says that at the time of her wedding, her father had passed down the tradition of giving the *Punjabi/sherwani* button, made up of gold attached with connected gold chain, to her husband. Her father had received the gift on his wedding day from his parents-

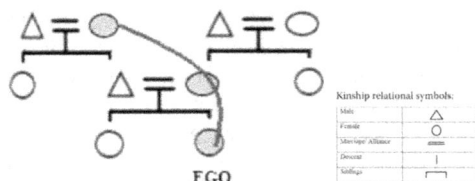

Figure 4.1 Symbolising the continuation of familial tradition.

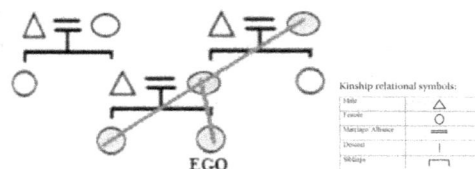

Figure 4.2 Symbolising the continuation of familial tradition.

in-law. So, her husband had passed down the same inherited gift to her daughter's husband as a family heirloom. This shows that gold jewellery is passed down as inheritance either through lineage or through marriage (see Figure 4.3).

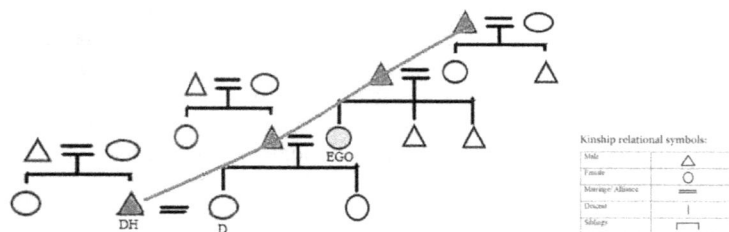

Figure 4.3 Illustrating a generational legacy.

Mrs S Talukdar, age 42, says that her husband has inherited a gold watch from her bilateral side. The following diagram (Figure 4.4) shows how inherited jewellery passes down to subsequent generations

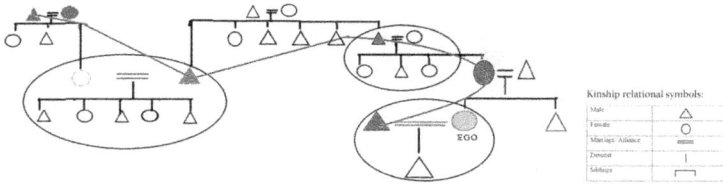

Figure 4.4 The interplay of family history, weddings and cherished legacies.

and plays the same role in continuing the tradition, i.e., gifting the gold watch to a son-in-law. Figure 4.4 shows that secondary's primary kin member, i.e., the mother's uncle (mother's father's elder brother), had received the gold wristwatch at the time of his wedding. He and his wife had passed down the gift, not to their children but to his primary kin, i.e., youngest brother at his wedding. Then the tradition follows the same trend to pass it to the next generation, that too on the female side.

This figure highlights that inherited jewellery can pass down to other primary kin members other than the decedent.

Inheritance of gold jewellery has been an expectation of an Indian bride at the time of her wedding. It poses a strong bond between the giver and the receiver of the jewellery. It is not a one-to-one relationship between two persons. It is the relationship which constructs the social value of giving (Veblen, 2005). Women are very fond of traditional designs and the ethnic values associated with them. The new, trendy designs are welcomed, but these types of jewellery are lightweight jewellery used for daily wear. The traditional jewellery is heavy and gorgeous, which every woman loves receiving as a gift. Passing down the heritage brings the element of emotion attached to the material object in the form of memories and stories of the earlier generation, which aids in strong social bonds. Therefore, gold jewellery as a material object manifests in stabilising and maintaining social relations (Berger, 2014, p. 65) to make the receiver feel incredibly special about herself/himself. It also expresses true love and gratefulness for having the person in their life. It strengthens the relationship by valuing the personal attachment between the giver and the receiver of the gifts (Berger, 2014, p. 78). Due to all this, gold jewellery is significantly continuing its value in maintaining the social relationship on one side, and on the other side, it is enhancing the social status of the giver as well as the receiver.

Consumers' Perceptions in Consumption of Gold Jewellery

The freedom of preferring jewellery initially starts within a family and then at the societal level. It has become a trend to purchase jewellery for fashion, highlighting status and class position. The Indian jewellery market, over the last 15 years, has mesmerised consumers through media with its overwhelming display of gold and diamond jewellery designs. It has helped to reproduce consumerism, where the consumers' psyche was ruled by the mediated image that acts as an umpire to instruct the consumers to lead a luxurious and secure life after purchasing gold jewellery. The arrival of corporate jewellers has given scope to the jewellery producers for trading massive jewellery collections by generating consumers' 'desire' for accumulating gold/diamond jewellery for building a 'society of consumers' (Bauman, 2007: 29) in India.

Mrs. K Baid, homemaker, aged 42, said, Gold jewellery has its novelty.

Mrs. J Guha, teacher, aged 50, said, The word jewellery itself hints at gold jewellery so I prefer gold jewellery over a diamond.

Mrs. M D Dutta, homemaker, aged 31, said, Gold jewellery is a convertible asset, at any given point of time it can be exchanged with cash or other gold jewellery depending upon the market value of the gold price.

Ms. P Mitra, assistant professor, aged 25, said, I prefer both but gold jewellery has a unique aesthetic essence that attracts me towards it. It is traditionally attached to our culture.

Ms. C Choudhury, assistant professor, aged 38, said, The golden colour of gold jewellery pleases my mind and the artistic decoration of each type of jewellery attracts my eyes to go for it. I love to wear gold bangle as it beautifies my hand after wearing it.

Mrs. S Raha, homemaker, aged 50, said, I belong to a middle-class category, and for us, gold is the most expensive metal that we can at least afford to buy. Diamond jewellery is for rich people, not for us. Pure diamond is very expensive and was not available in the market before the branded jewellery brought it into the market. The availability of diamond jewellery has become popular nowadays. Previously, only Tanishq used to sell diamond jewellery that too so expensive. Gold jewellery looks more beautiful than diamond jewellery. So, I prefer gold jewellery.

Mrs. B Jain, homemaker, aged 48, said, the interest rate offered by the bank is decreasing as the years proceed but the value of gold per gram has increased by more than double. It is worth buying gold jewellery as it fulfils the need to have ornament and side by side, it carries monetary value.

This illustrates that gold jewellery is culturally, religiously, aesthetically and financially more valuable than diamond jewellery. Wearing jewellery is a process of beautification of self that sooths the psyche of the consumer. Therefore, being a popular raw metal, gold is considered as the most auspicious metal in Hindu culture that enriches the heritage of ornamentation, signifies beautification and symbolises good luck to the wearer. Respondents who choose gold jewellery as their first preference express a similar view that gold jewellery symbolises purity. Its pure nature signalled the behaviour of people to 'touch gold' jewellery with their hand to ensure past or future. The consumption of gold jewellery is now a cultural phenomenon carried out historically through a popular culture where the psyche of the consumers is dependent upon day-to-day socialising processes that make them think it is a pure metal. Other than this, its economic value secures one's position in society. Universally, the acceptance of gold jewellery is associated with cultural and monetary value.

Persuasive Factors for Purchasing Gold Jewellery

The art of convincing consumers is a skill of the jewellers that helps them to attract customers towards their shop. This art hinges on certain factors that draw the attention of the consumers to a few attributes before purchasing jewellery. The stereotypical attributes for purchasing gold jewellery depend on design, price, purity, brand image, variety, display, promotional offers, resale, influence and services provided by the producer. Consumers' preference is categorised into Important, Neutral and Unimportant, which leads to an expression of 'freedom of choice'. The lifestyle and social status of a person relates to his or her preference for jewellery. Bauman has emphasised this as consumers' freedom of choice where they reproduce and re-alter their choices or preference before purchasing (Bauman, 1999: 38; Bauman, 2007: 84–85; Blackshaw, 2015: 121–122). In this era, people express their taste by articulating their 'freedom of choice' before buying, and this choice is governed by the commonality that leads them to identify themselves as a member of a certain class group. The consumers who have limited choice or no freedom of choice due to lack of wealth or any other reasons are unable to purchase jewellery, which gives them a 'subjective sense of insufficiency' and a lower social ranking. This subjective sense of the consumers cultivates self-lifestyle arising from a feeling of self-consciousness that is inculcated by the trendy jewellery designs popularised through social media. The primary survey, as depicted in chart 4.1, was used to gather data on the persuasive factors that lead consumers to purchase gold jewellery in India.

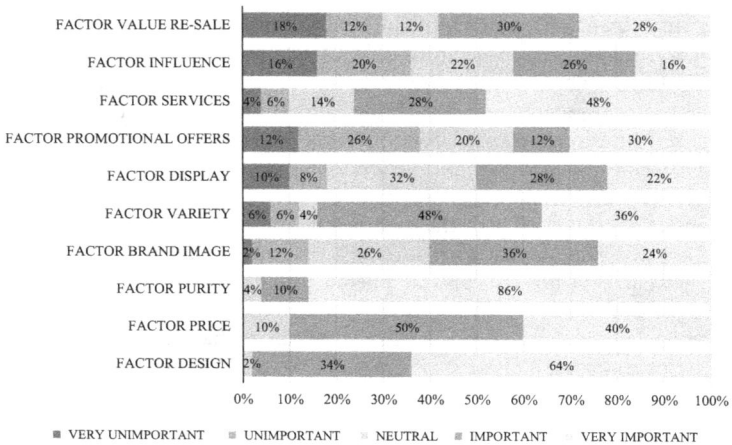

Chart 4.1 Factors for purchasing gold jewellery.

Source: Primary Survey September 2017 to August 2018.

Consumers often pay attention to the design worn by another person and wish to have the same jewellery design. Thus, the perception of 'design' governs the subjective preference, which affects the buying behaviour of the consumer. Consumers who consider design as 'very important' are adaptable and often pick different design elements when they cannot seem to discover the one they are looking for. Each design has its self-artistic appeal that drives the consumers to try to possess a unique jewellery design different from the others. In this case, consumers are of two types: first, those who want to replicate the same jewellery design; and second, those consumers who generally want to go for uniqueness. They either place special orders with traditional jewellers to have jewellery made that closely resembles the specific design they want to purchase, or they occasionally wait months to receive the jewellery from corporate jewellers as they are adamant about purchasing some specific design jewellery.

The consumer's behaviour in purchasing gold jewellery also oscillates with the price of gold. The 'very important' and 'important' category determines the purchasing capacity of the consumers that depend on the market value of the gold price, i.e., when the price is comparatively low consumers rush to the stores for purchasing jewellery. Also, the making charge/*mojuri* of the jewellery depends on the producer/*goldsmith's* ability to produce it at a certain cost. They keep a record of the fluctuating gold rates provided by the newspapers and other sources. The few consumers who are economically sound often purchase gold jewellery without paying any heed to the fluctuating gold rate in the market. This shows that willingness to purchase gold jewellery is determined by economic situation as well as the price of gold.

The value of gold does not always depend on the price; it depends on the purity of the product as well. Purity is guided by two factors: first, the KDM jewellery; and second, Hallmark Jewellery maintained by the BIS directed by the government. We know that at the present-day KDM jewellery is not considered the purest form of gold jewellery due to the potential health risks associated with the use of cadmium in the alloy. However, most of the local jewellers still use KDM jewellery as a cheaper alternative to Hallmarked jewellery. Additionally, the process of Hallmarking jewellery can be more costly and time-consuming, which may make KDM jewellery a more attractive option for some local jewellers. In this aspect, local jewellers are taking advantage of this ambiguity to earn profits when the consumers are unable to pay for hallmarked jewellery because the consumers lack the clarity of knowledge regarding the governmental policies for not buying KDM jewellery. Therefore, the consumers who consider purity as 'very important' purchase hallmarked jewellery for self-possession and for gifting. And those who consider 'Important', have the knowledge about Hallmark jewellery will be protected from being cheated by the jewellers. Still, they choose to buy KDM jewellery at the time of gift-giving, and for self-possession they buy hallmark jewellery.

It has been observed that the purchase of gold jewellery is correlated with the display of varieties of jewellery available in jewellery outlets. More varieties of jewellery will attract more consumers to the jewellery outlets. Thus, jewellery outlets trade on diversified forms of gold jewellery designed for almost every part of the body, such as ear, neck, nose, ankle, fingers, waist, arms, head, etc. And the art of making jewellery for a specific body part can also vary because there can be different styles, patterns and shapes of a particular type of jewellery.

It is observed that the 'variety' of gold jewellery is an 'important' factor that tempts the consumers to purchase jewellery from different outlets. And the jewellers (micro and macro entrepreneurs) are required to update their collections constantly, as the choices and preferences of the consumers also change with time. Today, consumers are witnessing changes in jewellery variations such as 'white gold' and 'rose gold' jewellery, produced by corporate jewellery showrooms; variations in the fusion of Indian and western style of jewellery is what the consumers seek. Purchasing jewellery is linked with emotions, and the jewellers focus on jewellery made up of contemporary designs, traditional designs, temple designs where gold is embedded and unique handcrafted gold jewellery (which is always in demand).

Another factor influencing the consumers after they enter the jewellery showroom/shop is the 'service' they receive from the sales representatives or conventional jewellers. Consumers who have received a good service from the jewellers tend to consider 'services' as an important factor before choosing a jewellery outlet. The service is not only limited to pre-purchase trial but also includes greeting the consumer, post-purchase availability of services like jewellery repair, exchange, resale, the time required for the making of jewellery and delivery, delivery at the doorsteps, greetings and communication over the phones. They prefer pre-purchase trial and post-purchase services more than other services. Corporate jewellers encourage customers to learn their own style before purchasing jewellery by offering pre-purchase jewellery samples both physically and online. Millennials prefer to purchase jewellery from those jewellery stores where they can first try out the jewellery. They also look for jewellery stores that offer cleaning, repairing and exchange services. Generally, the newer concept of luring the consumer by add on services does not usually affect the lower middle-class consumer's decision to purchase gold jewellery as they usually depend on their local family jewellers for any spectrum of jewellery-related works.

Moreover, giving promotional offers to the consumers is a common practice among all the jewellery stores, including corporate jewellers and middle-sized jewellers which helps them draw more consumers to their showroom. Consumers view promotional offer as a 'Very important' or 'Important' factor for visiting jewellery stores. They think that 'promotional offer' time is the perfect time to purchase gold jewellery at a good deal. This endorsement provided by the jewellery stores increases the jewellery sale during religious festivals and cultural occasions.

In addition to these highly significant factors, there are additional factors like possibility of resale, the influence of peers, display of jewellery and brand image that are less crucial for buying gold jewellery. The horizontal bar chart shows that consumers who choose 'brands' to help them establish a distinct identity. Brand gives a name to the product we purchase which represents a particular company trademark or company name, company logo or slogan. For example, Tanishq brand emphasises contemporary-designed diamond jewellery, providing trustable diamonds. The consumption of Tanishq jewellery is a marker of 'economically upper-class'. It is a sign of status and acts as an indicator of an elite lifestyle. With an increase in media exposure and awareness of fashion, the purview of all the companies to target rational consumer psychology by compelling them to choose their company for buying products has been widened. Consumers, on the other hand, are always in search of self-lifestyle to identify their existence into 'new selves' (Bauman, 2007, p. 115). Consumers have witnessed a change in the jewellery market with the growing number of corporate jewellery brands entering the market. This led to the shift of consumer base from the known reliable conventional jewellers to the flashy brand showrooms, which inversely changed the consumer's perception about the jewellery outlets. In contemporary society, a transition is noticed in terms of a factor for purchasing jewellery from product to brand image, where 'Brand' comes before product. The pace of this transformation is exceedingly fast. As a result, today's shoppers care more about the jewellery's brand than the store where it was purchased.

The resale value of gold jewellery is constantly assessed in terms of an emergency or financial crisis, but the likelihood of such a crisis is low. Jewellery is usually bought as an investment rather than solely for resale or influence. 'Resale value of jewellery' is an unimportant reason during purchase. The consumer's conscious mind does not think of investment or resale while purchasing jewellery. The concept of investment and the reason behind purchasing gold is psychologically transmitted to the minds of people, and hence they justify their purchase as an 'investment', which shows that there is resale value with the jewellery in future.

In spite of all the various tangible and intangible factors intertwined to motivate a consumer towards jewellery purchase, the final decision is always guided by the emotions and the captive value of gold. The demand for gold jewellery is always high. Both women and men wear gold jewellery to show their class and standard of life. However, buying jewellery is a personal choice, and this choice depends on the time when the consumers feel comfortable to purchase it. Chart 4.2 shows that the consumers prefer buying jewellery at the time of marriage. About 48 percent of consumers choose to purchase gold jewellery at the time of their marriage or to gift, followed by 28 percent of consumers who prefer to buy jewellery during their anniversary (for themselves and for giving gifts to the close members). There are certain months in the calendar where the lucky marriage dates are mentioned for conducting marriages in India. So, be it marriage season or anniversary day, the months remain the same year after year. Therefore, during those months, the consumers choose to buy gold jewellery. In other categories of purchase, consumers have given the reason as a sudden rise in the salary, sudden surprise gift for husband or wife, promotions or to make some day special.

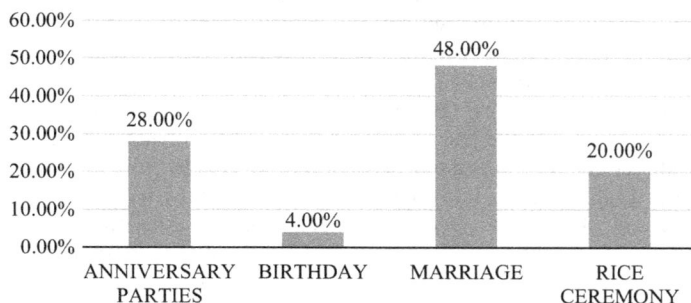

Chart 4.2 Occassions to wear gold Jewellery.

Source: Primary Survey September 2017 to August 2018.

However, the consumption of gold jewellery in India has faced challenges in recent years due to factors such as fluctuating gold prices, increasing competition from lightweight diamond jewelleries and changes in consumer preferences. Despite these challenges, gold jewellery consumption in India continues to be significant and is expected to remain so in the future. According to the 'Retail Gold Insight: India Jewellery' report from the World Gold Council, young women were active buyers of gold jewellery (33 percent belong to ages 18-24) in the years prior to 2019. So, there is a possibility that if the gold jewellery industry could be capitalising on consumer's desire for prestige and self-expressions then non-metropolitan places will also acquire the culture of metropolitan consumers. Urban Indians are more inclined towards the higher demands of gold jewellery than the rural consumers. They generally have more consumable income and are exposed to western culture more frequently than rural India, which has influenced their jewellery buying preferences and interests. Due to this, urban Indians are more inclined to choose contemporary gold jewellery designs that follow current trends in fashion.

Technology improvements, globalisation and the emergence of consumer culture are just a few of the elements that have contributed to this move towards a consumer-oriented society, where 18 carat and 14 carat gold jewellery has taken over the share of the jewellery market. This is particularly observed among the younger consumers. However, 22 carat gold jewellery has continued to dominate the Indian jewellery market, irrespective of local or regional variations. According to the World Gold Council's second quarterly report of 2022, there has been a year-on-year growth rate of 4 percent in the consumption of jewellery in India, which now amounts to 453.2 tonnes.

Note

1 It stands for Karatmeter Digital Measure. KDM, short for 'cadmium', is a type of gold alloy that is frequently used in India to make jewellery. Ninety-two and one-half percent pure gold and 7.5 percent cadmium, which serves as a binder, make up KDM gold. Because cadmium is a toxic metal that can be harmful to both human health and the environment, its use in KDM gold is debatable.

5   Challenges Before the Gold Jewellery Industry

Introduction

The Indian gold jewellery industry lacks a unified regulatory authority and therefore has to cope with numerous regulatory bodies and ministries that focus on various facets of policy issues. The members associated with the industry face challenges with numerous regulatory issues, fragmented markets and India's gold policies that are influenced by several governmental organisations. Governmental organisations that play a significant role in gold policies are detailed in Table 5.1 (Watal, 2018, p. 102).

The existence of several regulatory bodies and their rules make it challenging for the gold jewellery industry to implement all the policies, as it becomes difficult for them to face the numerous challenges related to raw gold metal, import duty, excise duty etc., which indirectly hinder the growth of the industry. Under the Ministry of Finance, a committee recommended the setting up of the 'Gold Board in India' as a unified institution for taking care of all the regulators. This will be managed by the RBI. It also recommended that GBI will set up a portal with 'Make in India in Gold' that provides all pertinent information relating to gold industry, government policies and programs on gold. Another proposal is to formulate a 'gold domestic control and bullion exchange' in India, which is still in its preliminary phase (see Table 5.2).

Governmental Gold Policies and Regulations

The gold jewellery industry and market are being influenced by the unpredictability of shifting gold policies. The governmental regulations and policies over the years that had a significant influence on the Indian gold market and jewellers are briefly described here:

• From the year 1947 to 1962, the possession of raw gold privately by an individual and the jewellery retailers were put under restrictions by banning private ownership of gold in order to regulate the gold supply, reduce gold smuggling and regulate the domestic price of gold.

DOI: 10.4324/9781032717951-5

Table 5.1 Governmental Organisations and Regulatory Bodies

Governmental Organisation	*Regulators*
Reserve Bank of India – regulates financial institutions, gold imports and distribution and holds India's gold reserves.	
Ministry of Finance	Department of Economic Affairs, Department of Financial Services, Department of Revenue Central Board of Direct Taxes Central Board of Excise and Customs Department of Expenditure Securities and Exchange Board of India Insurance and Regulatory Development Authority of India
Ministry of Commerce and Industry	Department of Commerce Department of Industrial Policy and Promotions (DPP) Directorate General of Foreign Trade Ministry of Consumer Affairs and Public Distribution (Bureau of Indian Standards) Ministry of Skill Development and Entrepreneurship Ministry of Labour- Directorate General of Employment and Training Ministry of Mines Ministry of Environment, Forests and Climate Change Ministry of MSME National Accreditation Board for Testing and Calibration Laboratories.

Source: Transforming India's Gold Market, NITI Aayog, Government of India, February 2018.

Table 5.2 Period-wise Major Reforms in Gold Policies

Year	*Periods*
1947–1962	Restriction Period
1963–1999	Prohibition Period
1990–2011	Liberalisation Period
2012–2013	Intervention Period
2014–2017	Transparency Period
2018 to till present	Assaying Period

Additionally, the government wanted people to stop buying gold in the forms of jewellery and coins; therefore the first gold bond scheme was established in India in 1962 in an effort to mobilise the gold jewellery and coins that the average person already owned with an exchange for new gold bonds.

- In 1963, Gold Control Rules were announced wherein the Government prohibited jewellery manufacturer or *karigars*/goldsmiths from making gold jewellery above 14 *carats* and initiated domestic trade for equal distribution of raw gold.
- In 1965, Gold Bond was introduced in an exchange of gold jewellery, gold coins and gold bars with an interest rate of 7 percent. National Defence Gold Bonds were introduced for 15 years where the interest rate was fixed at 2 percent for 10 grams of gold bars, coins and jewellery at 995 *purity*.
- In 1966, the 4th amendment of Defence of India Rules was declared to allow gold jewellery above 14 carats, but possession of gold bar was abolished. In the same year, the Gems & Jewellery Export Promotion Council was established. It is an apex body of gems and jewellery industry that promotes exports and products to international market.
- In 1968, the Gold Control Rules were clubbed under the Gold Control Act by which possession of gold bars by individuals became illegal; it became compulsory for jewellery retailers and gold refiners to have a license; and lastly, jewellery retailers needed to depend on the old scrapped gold as the metal for making new jewellery. Manufacturing of gold jewellery above 14 *carat* was prohibited, and it became mandatory for the jewellers to maintain a record for every transaction. Citizens could hold up to four kg of gold in the form of jewellery. These tremendous restrictions were put on jewellery retailers and citizens so that the purchasing of gold jewellery by consumers was reduced.
- In 1975, a Gold Auction Scheme was introduced through the Voluntary Disclosure of Income and Wealth Ordinance to encourage Indian families to reveal previously unreported wealth, including gold. This was done to prevent gold smuggling and to control the budget deficit.
- In 1990, the Gold Control Act was abolished because it failed to put a check on jewellery retailers since they were capable of operating their line of business with illegal (gold smuggling) means of getting new raw gold.
- In 1992, the Government of India permitted the import of raw gold and gold jewellery officially for the domestic market by formulating Non-Resident Indian (NRI) Schemes whereby an NRI could bring 5 kg of gold to India twice a year with a gap of six months; later in 1997, the limit was increased to 10 kg of gold. Till date, this NRI scheme is still in operation. This scheme has benefited jewellers by helping them run their businesses and trade successfully.
- In 1994 and 1997, the government introduced Special Import Licence (SIL) and Open General Licence Schemes (OGL). SIL is to expedite

entry of gold into India, and OGL Scheme has given official authorisation to 20 banks for the importation of gold.

- Since 1988, citizens can invest in the programs by purchasing five-year Gold Bonds.
- In 1999, the State Bank of India received authorisation to take gold from the public for earning interest (at a special interest rate) by introducing Gold Deposit Scheme (GDS).
- On April 11, 2000, the Bureau of Indian Standards (BIS) introduced Certification Schemes for Hallmarking of Gold Jewellery to put a check on the arbitrary rates set by the local and regional jewellers/goldsmiths in the name of the purity of gold. Conventional jewellers did not desire to use the governmental method to evaluate the purity of gold jewellery because they did not believe in the mechanical device for evaluating purity. Due to this, Government of India understood the essential need to spread consciousness among the gold jewellery consumers before buying gold. Buying gold in India has served its purpose for investment and as security money along with religious and cultural significance. For both the purposes, gold jewellery is a highly consumable product in India, so the government took the initiative on 26 November 1986 through a BIS act, and on April 1987, BIS started its activities to protect consumers from deceit and to protect the national economy. The Hallmarking Scheme under BIS provides 'third part assurance and satisfaction'[1] to the consumers to get 'right purity of gold (or silver) for the given price (value for money)' (Frequently Asked Questions on Hallmarking of Gold & Silver, 2018). This Scheme operates through Regional and Branch Offices of BIS located in various sections of the country. To open a Hallmarking Centre, a jeweller had to get recognition from BIS Assaying and Hallmarking Centres available in Regional Centres of the concerned state. The Indian Standard for gold is IS 1418.
- In 2002, banks were given permission to sell gold coins which saw an extension of this regulation to the Indian Post in 2008.
- Since November 2005, the Reserve Bank of India circulated 'Preferential treatment to Hallmarking Jewellery' to Banks 'while granting advances against jewellery' (Frequently Asked Questions on Hallmarking of Gold & Silver 2018).
- In March 2008, BIS launched Hallmarking on Silver Jewellery.
- In the 2012 Union Budget, a certain quantity of taxation was imposed on the purchase of gold jewellery above 2 lakhs. Customs duty was levied for the refinery and manufacturer of gold bars from 1 percent to 2 percent and Central Excise Duty was increased for gold bars, and gold ore, to 3 percent (GJEPC India, 2012)[2];

but later this increase in excise duty was withdrawn by the Government of India.

- In September 2013, the Government of India increased import duty on gold and platinum from 8 percent to 10 percent. Restrictions on the import of gold coins, sales through banks and offices, and reducing the maximum loan amount against gold from 75 percent to 60 percent were also introduced.
- In 2014, the World Gold Council indicated that India should launch 'Karigar Welfare Scheme' for the development of skills and training programmes for the jewellery *karigars* for showcasing Indian hand-made Jewellery (in this issue, 2014).[3] In 2014, the Government of India increased the import duty on gold and silver jewellery from 10 percent to 15 percent for protecting the domestic jewellery market by starting a project identified as 'Make in India'. The monetary value of gold and gold jewellery has increased in the domestic market after raising the import duty on gold, but the prising demand for handcrafted Indian-designed gold jewellery in the United States, Europe, China, Japan, particularly South Asian Countries has caused the government to focus on the exportation of handcrafted gold jewellery (Watal, 2018: 12–19) other than machine-made jewellery. The objective is to make India a worldwide manufacturing hub by recycling and refining of gold jewellery in order to boost the Indian gold jewellery market by exporting gold jewellery.
- In 2015, the Gold Deposit Scheme was withdrawn and introduced a new form as Gold Monetization Scheme with an objective to mobilise gold possessed by the citizens rather than depending on gold import. Afterwards, Gold Metal Loan (GML) and Gold Deposit Scheme was included in GMS. According to D'Souza (2015), commercial banks have financed jewellers to obtain gold under the GMS scheme which has allowed them to achieve their inventory targets. In this year, PAN (Tax number) became manda-tory for purchasing gold jewellery worth 2 lakhs and above. RBI lifted ban on import gold coins, medallions by trading houses and bank, and gave permission to provide gold on loan to the jewellers. National gold coin and Sovereign Gold Bond Scheme was also launched in this year in November.
- In the Union Budget of 2016–2017, the Government of India re-imposed the excise duty of 1 percent on jewellers without CENVAT credit or 12.5 percent with CENVAT credit with mandatory require-ment of PAN card for transactions of 2 lakhs or above. Hallmarking jewellery has been revised, allowing the jewellery to be hallmarked at 22 carats instead of the previously mandated higher carat value. TCS (Tax collected at source) is also imposed on transactions above a specific threshold amount where the policy has been revised from

a 1 percent TCS on purchases of gold jewellery worth 2 lakhs or above to a 1 percent TCS on purchases of 5 lakhs or above. In November 2016, the government demonetised ₹500 and ₹1000 notes for removing the black money from Indian Market, and 3 percent of GST and 1 percent of VAT were imposed[4]. In 1st of January 2017, a New Bureau of Indian Standard (BIS) Act was introduced.

• According to a new regulation from 2018, any accredited assaying and hallmarking centre may establish an offsite facility in compliance with the bureau's guidelines, where the centre will be in charge of determining the purity and fineness of the gold metal items it has hallmarked. Additionally, the Centre must notify the Bureau whenever there is a change in the Centre's administration, location, name or address.

• On June 16th 2021, Bureau of Indian Standard (BIS) has introduced mandatory hallmarking on six forms of purities of gold jewellery: 14 *carat*, 18 *carat*, 20 *carat*, 22 *carat*, 23 *carat* and 24 *carat*, with a motive to focus on the variation of jewellery design and consumers preferences. BIS also issued a declaration that from June 2022 jewellers cannot sell gold jewellery that is not hallmarked, regardless of purity i.e., every piece of gold jewellery, regardless of its carat weight, would need to be legally hallmarked.

Response to the Governmental Policies and Regulations

The governmental policies on gold (as raw material), gold jewellery and jewellery trade have impacted the jewellers and the unorganised gold jewellery industry adversely. The responses from the industry came in the form of challenges.

Hallmarking versus KDM Dilemma

Jewellers organised a national strike in 2012 to protest new laws to safeguard the gold jewellery industry. In March 2012, The Central Board of Excise under the Ministry of Finance declared its new policy to introduce 'Excise Duty' on gold bars, gold coins and gold jewellery. By a policy decision made by Shri Pranab Mukherjee (the then finance minister), the gold artisans or conventional jewellers would have to pay 0.3 percent of excise duty, which meant 30 paisa duty on ₹100 transaction. The nitty-gritty in maintaining a financial record for every transaction of selling jewellery was thought to be tough for local and regional jewellers; they also apprehended harassment at the hands of the excise department. The small traders were completely ignorant about the processes of doing accounting and maintaining tax files.

Following Budget 2012, in which the declaration was made, the jewellers went on a Nation-wide strike because they thought it would be difficult for them to follow the complexities of this excise duty and particularly when they have to pay value-added tax (VAT). Another important reason for them was that if they had to pay 0.3 percent extra on transactions the jewellery prices would increase, which would have an adverse financial impact on their business. Since they deal with small capital, and their business being small, the new changes in the policy created a lot of apprehensions. Conventional jewellers expressed their worries by saying that it was a trap of the government to impose 0.3 percentage of every transaction because the government knew that the jewellery industry was run by uneducated and less educated people whose livelihood depended on their hand skills; any legal or formal or mandatory rule imposed on them by the government would make them handicapped in maintaining financial records. For maintaining financial record for every transaction, they would have to hire the services of cost/ chartered accountants, which would mean extra cost. As an outcome of all-India strike, Government had to withdraw the proposed excise duty and reduce the tax on imported gold, which the government had increased by 4 percent.

In 2016 Budget, Finance Minister Shri Arun Jaitley proposed levying 1 percent of excise duty again on non-silver jewellery, especially on gold jewellery. He also made it mandatory to use PAN card for a jewellery purchase worth ₹ 2 lakh and above. The proposal reflected the fact that the financial department country was trying to put some regulations on the gold transactions in order to generate revenue. The government was aware of the volume of jewellery trade in India. India was the largest consumer of gold before China took over in 2013; about 974.8 tonnes of gold consumption in India come from either imports or recycling. It was also observed that gold consumption in India holds the highest position in the world as a percentage of GDP (Menon, 2015). But such regulations on every transaction on 'gold' brought trouble for jewellers all over India. It was found that within three days of the National strike in 2016, more than 300 associations, small and medium-sized jewellers, goldsmiths and many more persons, directly or indirectly linked with jewellery business in India, participated in the strike.[5] They supported the National strike by organising candlelight rally against Central Excise Duty on March 13th, 2016 with a slogan '*inspector raj cholbena cholbena*', '*hamare mange puri karo*', '*roll back excise duty*'. A news item on 18th day of the strike calculated that the strike had caused a loss of ₹ 60,000–70,000 crore to the jewellery industry in India. This made the government re-think about the imposed rules and declared that there will be no 'inspector raj', which means jewellers will not face any harassment from excise officers or 'inspector raj'.[6]

National Strike 2012 and 2016

The mandatory 'Hallmarking on gold' has also adversely impacted the small-sized jewellers because the process involves additional cost and administrative hassles as the hallmarking centre was previously available only in the central cities of India, such as Lajpat Nagar, Kolkata, Jaipur City, Trissur, etc. During the initial phase after introduction of Hallmark jewellery, the middle class and upper middle class who were aware of this government policy started buying gold ornaments that were made and sold by the corporate jewellery houses, as they were able to provide Hallmarked jewellery. The conventional jewellers were unable to offer hallmarked certificate of the purity of gold jewellery because they had to travel to the hallmarking centre, which was in centre of the city. The cost of travel was becoming an additional burden for small-sized jewellers and *karigars* directly affecting their ability to make a profit as well as being unable to hold the trust of the consumers who preferred hallmark jewellery. They tried to persuade consumers to believe in KDM jewellery because it formerly dominated the market before hallmarking became a rule. However, low-income jewellers and goldsmiths have claimed that the local hallmarking centre is biased when it comes to applying the hallmark on gold jewellery. They felt that there must be significant corruption at the local hallmarking level because the central hallmarking centres seldom ever conduct thorough investigations in the local level. They also suggested that when government is thinking about consumer safeguards for checking the purity of gold then why did not the government open a proper carat verification centre for the consumers where they may examine their jewellery before and after sale. The dilemma between the hallmark and KDM jewellery among the jewellers and within the consumers had divided the consumers. This shift in consumer preference towards corporate branded jewellery showrooms or middle-sized jewellers has put a cost on the petty small-sized jewellers and *karigars*.

Moreover, a new jewellery consumer culture along with hallmark jewellery has also emerged over the past 15 years, where wearing jewellery with the company's name (brand) on it has become fashionable and adds more value to the ornaments. This provided an impetus for the middle and upper classes consumers to abandon the traditional and petty jewellery traders in order to shift towards the big branded corporate jewellery showrooms (Sennettle, 2006). The opportunity to open hallmarking centres in numerous cities and towns has been made possible by mandatory hallmarked jewellery regulations effective from 2021. Out of 748 districts, 256 districts in India have opened hallmarking centres where 130,205 jewellers have registered with BIS (Pessemier et al., 2022). Even the BIS data for 2022 shows that 1349 recognised hallmarking centres are successfully operating at the local and regional levels. This availability of the hallmarking centres at local and regional levels has benefitted the jewellers and goldsmiths as they need to make a short trip to the nearby district to get their jewellery hallmarked. Their efforts and trip budget have decreased so they sincerely appreciate the governmental decision for hallmarking of jewellery.

Impact of Demonetisation

The shortage of cash has a strong influence on the demand for gold jewelleries. News regarding restrictions on gold possession and gold jewellery transactions exacerbated the situations because people having liquid cash of Rs 500 and Rs 1,000 were ready to purchase any forms of gold jewellery (irrespective of jewellery shops) as a result of converting black money into white in the form of assets. This sudden rise in demand contributed to acceleration of gold prices, i.e., the gold price for 10 grams of gold rose to ₹30,050 (Siliguri metropolitan city, West Bengal, gold market price in November 2016) but on the day of demonetisation the price rose to anything between ₹37,000 and ₹43,000. Each customer was ready to buy jewellery by giving an advance of ₹ 2 lakhs to Rs 4 Lakhs. A medium-sized jeweller, aged 41, told me that on the demonetisation night, some consumers had exchanged banned rupees with gold jewellery for lower values, they accepted Rs 950 for 1,000 notes. It was found that between November 8th and November 12th 2016, all the conventional jewellers made a huge profit out of sudden rise in sales following demonetisation. Following this chaos, the government had forced the bullion dealers/traders to close their business for a few days. Consumers who did panic buying jewellery mostly belonged to business class and the upper class. Although demonetisation has been impacted by unorganised small and medium-sized jewellers, it has also pushed the jewellery industry to adopt digitalisation in transactions (Google Pay and Paytm using QR code) and online purchases. also, the use of UPI transactions (Unified Payment Interface) in July 2022, as per World Gold Council.

Impact of Goods and Service Tax

Before the implementation of the Goods and Service Tax (GST) in 2017, jewellers and goldsmiths involving in unorganised manufacturing units were kept away from the service tax and compliance net. The imposition of GST on all gold transactions had increased the worries of the small traders during the initial phase. The usage of GST and the associated process has benefitted business transactions and have decreased business cost because different states in India used to have distinct tax structures, which had an impact on the consumers' purchasing power. Prior to GST, jewellers relied on a variety of distributive channels, such as utilising their own gold metal to make jewellery (see Chapter 3), but nowadays every distributive channel uses a distinct transaction to keep an official record of the transaction data. This shows that the transaction process has been streamlined so that jewellers can directly purchase their own bullion and transfer it for the production and sale of jewellery. Additionally, it has given bullion dealers the chance to launch online services that make it simpler for jewellers and goldsmiths to make purchases as it offers transparency in pricing. The corporate jewellers with their better management skills have adjusted to the new legislations well quite quickly. But the small jewellers had a tough time adjusting. This reveals that GST has benefitted the jewellers (bullions, traders, manufacturer, retailers, wholesalers) and consumers in transparency in pricing and purity of gold.

The ability to manage a small manufactured jewellery shop at a low cost is still a concern for small-sized jewellers and goldsmiths, but medium-sized jewellers have hired skilled employees to comply with GST accounting and maintaining necessary documentation. Corporate jewellers, whether they are branded or unbranded, have a 5–10 percent increase in staff and system requirements, in the view of Ashish Pethe, Chairman of Gems and Jewellery Council (GJC) India (Pessemier et al., 2022). As a result of the fragmented nature of the sector, 86,000 jewellers have registered for GST taxes; these registered jewellers are anticipated to generate annual revenues of at least Rs 4 million (US$50,000) each. This shows that the gold jewellery industry is progressing.

Impact of COVID-19

The coronavirus COVID-19) pandemic has not only affected Indian economy but has left an impact on the gold jewellery industry. Due to concern over the spread of the virus, the industry witnessed fewer customers during the typical jewellery-buying seasons. On the other hand, there were people who had to sell their gold jewellery just to sustain their life when covid ceased their daily source of earnings. The Reserve Bank of India (RBI) announced a new policy on August 6, 2020, increasing the LTV (loan-to-value) ratio for gold loan lenders (whether they are banks or non-banking financial corporations) from 75 percent to 90 percent of the value of the gold jewellery (Sinha, 2020). All the banks and major bullion traders welcomed this RBI regulation because it made it easier for them to make personal or corporate loan payments. They can also request for a loan against the same amount of gold at a higher interest rate. The large jewellery traders have benefited from this.

However, it had a detrimental effect on the lower-paid gold jewellers and the general public because they were unable to repay the loan during the crisis time (Madhukalya, 2021). As an outcome, many small-sized jewellers gave up their hereditary jewellery business. The gold jewellery industry, however, never loses hope that they will overcome all of these obstacles once the situation with COVID improves. Due to the pandemic, both online and offline buying have expanded. Consumers now shop virtually before making in-person purchases or sending gifts to loved ones.

Issues that Gold Jewellery Industry Is Facing

The conventional jewellers are currently dealing with a variety of issues in maintaining their business. Some of these issues have their roots in outside events that are rooted in the external complex regulations and dominant corporate jewellers. The essence of the jewellery industry is capital-intensive so the conventional jewellers are left depending on their inherent skills which adds more challenges for maintaining the jewellery business. The issues that gold jewellery industry is facing as a challenge are:

a The current jewellery manufacturing industries rely heavily on automation that is rapidly replacing the processes employed in jewellery creation for polishing, dyeing, manufacturing and designing. It has been found that in today's market, intermediaries offer pre-assembled jewellery components that may be combined to make jewellery that has been shown to be an efficient approach to cut production costs. The small-sized jewellers do not have the resources to purchase them in bulk, but the middle-sized jewellers do. To solve this issue, a few conventional jewellers located in common locality come together to buy ready-made jewellery components that they then share among the small-sized jewellers and goldsmiths in accordance with their respective demands. This is destroying the artistic skills of crafting and limiting their ability to be creative while making jewellery. Similar designs are becoming prevalent and the traditional method of making jewellery is slowly fading away. At the end, it is creating a situation where the conventional jewellers are unable to sustain their jewellery business because there is a lack of individuality in the pattern of art.

b The heart of the gold jewellery industry is the goldsmith. They are able to create jewellery based on any instructions provided by the customers, but they are experiencing difficulties because jewellery designs are becoming more complex and mixed. Due to the limitations of their talents, out-dated tools and conventional community-based skills, they are unable to adapt to new needs. The new methods of creating jewellery poses the risk of turning the traditionally trained goldsmiths into little more than makers of assembled pieces. They feel cut off from their long-honed skill of jewellery creation because their craft is no longer useful. Even while local consumers still choose traditional designs over modern designs, it is getting harder for traditional jewellers to adapt with shifting consumer tastes into light-weight jewellery. The majority of small-sized jewellers and goldsmiths find contemporary jewellery designs and patterns appealing, but they are unable to produce the fashionable current designs when they are in style. The trend vanishes from the market until they can recreate such styles because they lack design-based innovation. Until they can recreate such designs, the fashion disappears from the market. In parallel, the *karigars* employed by conventional jewellers do not get the proper credit (pay) or recognition (proper making charge) that the shop owner demands from the clients for creating each item of jewellery.

c The slow growth of the unorganised gold jewellery industry has persuaded all jewellers to motivate their offspring to go for other career options rather than continuing with their hereditary business. Many goldsmiths and small-sized jewellers are faced with the threat of losing job cause of traditional skills and lack of current knowledge, and the ones who continue to work are paid less. A gripping sense of alienation has forced many goldsmiths to leave the job as *karigar* and to start a new business of their own outside jewellery business. Therefore, a feeling of alienation leads to a feeling of marginalisation. The experience of marginality among the small-sized jewellers and goldsmiths are generated after the growth of corporate jewellers in Indian jewellery market, as their entry has helped to diversify the monopoly hereditary business of the *swarnakars*. Since then, many of the local jewellers and *karigars* have experienced the feeling of marginalisation specifically in three main contexts: the workplace, the family and last, the social milieu. These three segments are intertwined with one another in such a way that when one area is affected, then other areas will automatically get impacted. Overall, this has adversely affected the conventional jewellers, especially the small-sized jewellers and goldsmiths; and in overall the gold jewellery industry.

d The shortage of permanent goldsmiths is affecting the small and middle-sized jewellery industry. It has become a frequent pattern in the gold jewellery industry for the young, motivated goldsmiths to open their own businesses after becoming proficient in the craft and techniques of jewellery production (from the shop owner and other goldsmiths). Side by side, an intra-generational job mobility is found among conventional jewellers where they capture some of the dependable customers of their former business. This is leading to increased competition among the small-sized jewellery industries where they employ staff or manufacture based on contracts. As a result, small-sized jewellery industries are fragmented and scattered and growing in numbers.

e The alienation of goldsmiths and jewellers can be stopped if a suitable training facility is set up for the traditional jewellers to operate the business. The goldsmiths and the people associated with gold jewellery industry must receive specialised training for creating modern jewellery using contemporary tools but the training institutes in India are located only in Mumbai, Delhi, Jaipur and Surat. The GJEPC (Gem and Jewellery Export Promotion Council) oversees these training facilities to ensure that the gold jewellery sector maintains the highest level of technical proficiency in Computer-Aided Design (CAD) and Computer-Aided Manufacturing (CAM). This technical expertise has encouraged competition among goldsmiths who work for large or medium-sized jewellery companies with well-known trademarks. The small-sized gold jewellery industries are unable to enrol in those trainings because they are unaware of government schemes and yojanas related to skill development programmes; even if they are made aware of these programmes by their local jewellery associations, they will be unable to do so because they lack the necessary credentials and qualifications. Their biggest barrier has been their inability to pay the registration fees, which has prevented them from enroling and registering for these programmes. The local, regional and national jewellery associations must take up the task of modernising the industry in order to survive in a competitive market. It is found that the middle-sized gold jewellery industries are updated about these training programmes and certification course for running and sustaining the goldsmiths in the shop. According to Mr A. Agarwal, Mr P. Karmakar, Mr M. Saraf (conventional jewellers) and many more middle-sized jewellers have acknowledged the importance of specialised training and modernisation for the survival of the business. They have participated in various training programmes held in Kolkata, Delhi and Mumbai, and have been immensely benefitted. Mr. A. Agarwal was of the view that the small-sized jewellers and goldsmiths are largely unaware of all these programmes and the few of them who are aware are educationally backward, some of them have no interest to attend, some are afraid to participate and most of them feel that it is not for them. Conventional jewellers who are less educated were ignorant about up-gradation training and were unable to acquire information about the programmes. These training programmes are expensive and are held outside regional level, so they were unable to pay the course fee for training purpose. This gap in knowledge and lack of awareness has created problems for small-sized jewellery industry and gold manufacturing industry.

f Work life for goldsmiths is significantly influenced by their workplace. The majority of the goldsmith's working life is spent there. It is natural that the goldsmiths' quality of life, physical health and mental state would be directly impacted by the size and physical environment of the workshop. It is observed that at least one *karigar* is kept in the workshop by small jewellery store owners. For them, a basic workshop is around 5 feet by 5 feet in size. The usual room size in medium-sized shops, where 6–7 people are employed, is 9 feet by 10 feet. Besides congestion, the work involves flame, burner, high temperature resulting from heating and melting the gold. Fresh air does not flow in the absence of windows and ceiling fans. The working environment becomes intolerable due to rising heat, irritating smoke and smell of the chemicals used for melting gold. For cooling the temperature of the room, they use table fan. While the work is on, the goldsmiths are not allowed to use a fan as it interferes with the process of making jewellery. The goldsmiths and petty-bourgeois jewellers undergo mental and physical anguish in the workshop due to inadequate ventilation and contaminated air, which causes exhaustion and drowsiness. They are subjected to breathing in harmful dust all day long, which damages their health permanently. In general terms, this can be termed hazardous occupation, but from the perspective of the *karigars*, it is 'taken-for-granted realm of routine' (Storey, 2014). The study shows that 82.3 percent are affected by asthma and spondylitis. Other 17.64 percent have developed eye problems. In this way, the goldsmiths/gold makers or petty-bourgeoise jewellers are susceptible to many health issues. They develop different ailments in hands, arms, neck, shoulder, and back. These concerns have made it challenging for them to continue to work in this field of business, and it has been proven that their decision to leave has become a key factor for those involved in diverse occupations.

• The biggest challenge confronted by the conventional jewellers is access to capital and lack of long-term family assets for infrastructure investments because their primary focus is on buying gold for the production of jewellery rather than spending money (investment) on infrastructural expenditure. Due to the lack of proper infrastructural and e-commerce facilities, local jewellers and goldsmiths are facing competition from regional and national jewellers. Additionally, acquiring bank financing is another challenge for small-sized jewellers and goldsmiths as they frequently rely on the monthly gold plan, money lenders and the income earned from the sale of any jewellery product (Pessemier et al., 2022). They are unable to manage the financial parts of the business because they deal primarily with cash and reliable cash from the consumer, which immediately hinders business growth.

These are some of the major challenges that traditional jewellers deal with, along with a lack of funding, a lack of imagination and vision and an antiquated production method. As a result, they lose their heirloom clients when a large firm enters the market and offers all of its benefits. Presently, consumers are digitally and technologically enabled in purchasing gold jewellery from companies' websites. The middle-sized jewellers have managed to retain their hold on a space in the market as they resort to different kind of business strategies to retain their traditional customers coming primarily from the lower and middle classes. The gold jewellery industry has witnessed that the millennials are opting for gold jewellery as a feasible practise for investment. But the small-sized jewellery industry and manufacturing units are unable to take any financial risks by investing in individual business. Instead for producing for reinvestment and reproduction, they rely on the pre-capitalist mode of production to supply their necessities. Sanyal refers to this as a 'need-economy' (Sanyal, 2019:216). The workers in the gold jewellery industry desire their son to choose a different career because it is very challenging to maintain the business despite the difficulties in accessing finance, fluctuating gold price with market trends, changing gold policies and regulations and increasing dependency on gold bullion/traders.

Notes

1 Frequently Asked Questions on Hallmarking of Gold & Silver, Retrieved June 9, 2018, (http://www.bis.org.in/cert/FAQsHM.pdf)
2 Highlights of Union Budget 2012–2013, March 19, 2012, Retrieved March 2, 2015 (https://gjepc.org/admin/Circulars/1229521255_Circular-to-all-Members-on-Budget2012-13.pdf)
3 Weekly Economic Bulletin. September 30-October 06, 2014. Retrieved March 4, 2016, (http://indiainbusiness.nic.in/newdesign/upload/Publications/Weekly/Oct_2014/MEA_Newsletter%20Sept_30_Oct_06.pdf)
4 Government imposes 1 percent excise duty on gold jewellery, Deccan Chronicles with Agency Inputs,
    Published on March 1, 2016, Retrieved June 6, 2018 https://www.deccanchronicle.com/nation/current-affairs/010316/government-reimposes-1-per-cent-excise-duty-on-gold-jewellery.html)
5 Jewellers begins 3 Days Pan-Strike to Protest Excise Duty Levy. (2016, March 02). Retrieved March 03, 2016 (www.ndtv.com).

6 Indo-Asian News Service on April 3 2016, 6:36 PM in New Delhi presented a new flash with a headline Excise Duty will bring back Inspector Raj: Arvind Kejriwal, highlights 'The excise duty ... will give rise to corruption. The excise inspectors will ask for bribe from the jeweller .... when the United Progressive Alliance government was in power, Pranab Mukherjee as the Union Finance Minister had also introduced the same tax in 2012. However, the then Congress led government had to roll back the tax after resistance from jewellers. The President also agreed with the view that it will bring the Inspector Raj back in the country'. Indo-Asian News Service. Retrieved April 3, 2016 (www.india.com).

Conclusion

The gold jewellery industry in India has witnessed a remarkable transformation, seamlessly merging the richness of traditional practices with the finesse of exquisite craftsmanship, while embracing the winds of modernisation. Ancient civilisations laid the foundation for intricate designs and the use of precious gemstones, while the Mughal era brought Persian and Central Asian influences to jewellery patterns. The British colonial introduced fusion fashion and standardised production techniques. The post-independence period witnessed a resurgence of traditional techniques and the rise of renowned corporate-branded jewellery houses. Today, the gold jewellery industry combines traditional craftsmanship with contemporary designs and uses technology for accuracy and efficiency. This evolution has extended its influence to diverse facets of the industry, encompassing production, design, distribution and the overall consumer experience. The juxtaposition of age-old traditions and modern advancements have brought about significant changes, shaping the landscape of the gold jewellery industry in India. The industry has adapted to meet the demands of a dynamic market, while continuing to preserve the essence of its cultural heritage. This book delves into the multifaceted journey of the Indian gold jewellery industry, unravelling the impact of its evolution and the interplay between tradition and modernity. It encompasses various dimensions, including cultural identity, social status, gender dynamics and social bonds.

This book tries to take the reader on a journey through the world of gold consumption and the enchanting realm of Indian gold jewellery. It has explored the global factors that drive the demand for gold, including population expansion, urbanisation and economic volatility. The role of central banks and consumer demand for gold jewellery has also been highlighted as influential factors that contribute to the rise in gold prices. As a powerful symbol of identity and heritage, gold jewellery serves to connect individuals with their lineage, preserving ancestral traditions

DOI: 10.4324/9781032717951-6

and reflecting the rich cultural tapestry of India. Its implication is particularly evident in pivotal life events such as weddings and religious ceremonies, where gold jewellery holds a central position, reinforcing the spiritual and cultural fabric of Indian society. In addition to its cultural significance, gold jewellery plays a crucial role in empowering women, providing them with a means to express their individuality and agency. It serves as an emblem of personal style and serves to enhance authentic selves. Furthermore, gold jewellery serves as a means for social interactions and strengthens community bonds, especially during festivals and celebratory occasions. These events provide opportunities for people to come together, gift jewellery and celebrate their shared heritage and traditions.

The industry in India is predominantly characterised by the presence of informal traditional jewellers. The artisans and small-scale businesses have been the backbone of the jewellery industry for centuries, carrying forward the legacy of intricate craftsmanship and traditional techniques. Unlike large-scale, formalised jewellery businesses, these informal jewellers often operate in family owned businesses or small workshops, relying on their inherited knowledge and skills. Their skills and techniques are learned through apprenticeships and are passed down within families or communities, thus ensuring the continuity of craftsmanship. This process of socialisation and cultural transmission is integral to the industry's reliance on skilled artisans and the preservation of traditional jewellery-making practices.

For these reasons, they possess a deep understanding of local traditions, cultural preferences and regional designs, allowing them to cater to the diverse tastes and preferences of the Indian population. They have the expertise role as specialised workers and craftsmanship necessary for intricate jewellery makings, such as designing, stone setting, engraving and filigree work. Their skills are highly valued, and their division of labour ensures the production of high-quality jewellery. Their expertise enables them to create high-end customised jewellery. For this reason, these conventional jewellers have built strong relationships with their customers, often serving multiple generations within the same families. This trust and personal connection have been nurtured over time, reinforcing consumer loyalty and modifying business.

However, in recent years, the industry has witnessed a notable shift as a result of the emergence of corporate-branded jewellers, technological advancements in jewellery making and the influence of globalisation. The rise of organised jewellery retail chains and branded jewellery outlets with an e-commerce platform offers consumers a wide range of choices and convenience when making purchases. This shift towards organised retail has contributed to increased standardisation, transparency and adherence to governmental regulations pertaining to gold jewellery. As a result, conventional jewellers face challenges in meeting these new consumer expectations in terms of shopping experience, product quality and transparency. And conventional jewellers are compelled to reassess their business and marketing strategies, including upgrading their jewellery stores to remain competitive in the evolving market.

As the world becomes more inter-connected, cultural boundaries blur and globalised consumer culture can lead to homogenisation of jewellery preferences (like lightweight jewellery and machine-made [CAD/CAM] homogenised jewellery design). This may lead to culturally hybridised jewellery in one aspect, and in another aspect, it may lead to a disconnection between individuals and their cultural lineage. Thus, Zygmunt Bauman's theory on Liquid modernity provides a lens through which one may view traditional jewellery-making businesses that not only face challenges but also persist in response to the changing circumstances. For example, corporate jewellers, backed by substantial financial resources, were unable to target the regional jewellery marketplace as they find difficulties in offering diverse community (culture-wise) jewellery. So in order to spread their wings at the regional level, they presented opportunities for collaboration and partnership with conventional jewellers. Few conventional jewellers have found avenues for growth and expansion by joining hands with corporate jewellers. Therefore, we can see that the gold jewellery industry in India is gravitating towards automation and mass manufacturing, enabling producers to satisfy the rising demand for jewellery across regional, national and worldwide markets. This development not only allows for expanding the conventional jewellery businesses but also helps to meet the evolving needs and preferences of consumers.

Over time, the gold jewellery industry in India is therefore moving towards automation and mass manufacturing, enabling producers to satisfy the rising demand for jewellery across regional, national and worldwide markets. It has also experienced notable shifts in adapting to changing consumer preferences and market dynamics. However, traditional jewellery-making techniques and craftsmanship can struggle to adapt and survive in rapidly changing cultural demands. But then again, the fusion of traditional craftsmanship and modern design sensibilities has broadened the industry's appeal to a diverse range of consumers, including the younger generation. Many consumers still value heritage, intricate conventional aesthetic designs and hand-made jewellery (personal touch) associated with conventional jewellers, leading to continued demand for their products.

In Indian society, corporate jewellery production is no longer centrally planned; rather, it is dispersed among several divisions and is thus opaque. The neoliberal system, which thrives on fostering consumption, is now the centre of attention. The society is now stratified according to degrees of consumption. The consumer market flourishes by absorbing cultural values and ideologies and by constantly enticing the public by conjuring up impossible fancies and desires. The gold jewellery industry thrived on creating fresh fantasies and aspirations (Bauman, 2007, 1999). It is debatable if customers have any agency and are fully unaware of the business-men's cognitive tricks. This cannot simply be answered with 'yes' or 'no'. Consumers in the poor and lower middle classes may not have much extra money to spend on gold jewellery unless it is absolutely necessary (occasion specific). These consumers may also not be as interested in deciphering the complex business strategies of the jewellery industry, as their prime focus is on purity and traditional designs. On the other side, the educated and enlightened consumer who has the money and motivation to invest in gold jewellery is aware of the business models and operating procedures of the commodity market, but they are unable to counteract the allure of the commodities and either unconsciously or consciously yield to the demands of the contemporary market.

As for the future, the Indian jewellery industry is expected to continue its growth rate. Rising disposable incomes, urbanisation and an ex-panding middle class are likely to drive the demand for gold jewellery. Additionally, the increasing influence of social media and e-commerce platforms will play a significant role in shaping consumer preferences and purchasing patterns, which will adversely affect the conventional gold jewellery industry; but by adapting technological advancement while preserving the traditional knowledge,[1] they can find a balance between tradition and contemporary demands. Conventional jewellers have long-standing relationships with consumers because they rely on word-of-mouth consumer's recommendations. Their traditional knowl-edge contributes significantly to their cultural capital (Bourdieu, 1986) which differentiates from corporate capital. And it influences their position and reputation within the Indian jewellery industry. In this process, conventional jewellers can capitalise on their unique craftman-ship, cultural authenticity, linkages to community jewellery designs and personalised consumer services. As a result, conventional jewellers are able to create a niche market by providing distinctive and meaningful narratives that appeal to consumers who appreciate authenticity and cultural significance. However, corporate-branded jewellery houses have substantial cultural capital due to their brand identities, marketing strategies and latest trend in jewellery. They can influence consumers' approaches to purchasing jewellery through advertisements and promo-tional offers, which develop market domination attributed to this cultural capital. But the manufacturing of jewellery in India has changed from traditional artistry to a synthesis of old and new methods. Innovation in design, technical development, sustainability and individualised preferences will shape the industry's future. The industry is well-positioned to satisfy the evolving needs of consumers and maintain development in the upcoming years by embracing these trends.

In the neoliberal system, modern capitalism survives by encouraging consumers to make purchases. A large portion of these purchases are made in reaction to artificial compulsions induced by society and stoked by marketing that affect consumers' minds. The brand names give the decorations additional worth, which is frequently fictitious. The conventional jewellers, on the other hand, are well-prepared to take advantage of the social and cultural spaces that gold jewellery possesses. They are also well-prepared to take advantage of seasonal hikes in the demand for gold jewellery, along with the feelings of the general population. Even though the jewellery business has clearly undergone a major transformation as a result of the rise of corporate-branded jewellery companies, it does not necessarily mean the end of the conventional jewellery industry.

Note

1 Have a deep understanding of the cultural symbols, motifs and design elements specific to their regional or community-based jewellery styles and expertise in selecting and combining precious metal, gemstones and other materials to design a jewellery also contributes to the uniqueness of their creation. This knowledge allows them to create jewellery that resonates with cultural traditions and carries a distinct identity.

References

Adorno, T. (1991). *The Culture Industry*. London and New York: Routledge.
Adorno, T., & Horkeimer, M. (1972). *Dialectic Enlightenment*. (J. Cumming, Trans.) New York: The Seabury Press.
Arantola, H. (2002). *Consumer Bonding – A Conceptual Exploration*. Journal of Relationship, *1*(2), 93–107.
Atei, G., Rezaei, F., & Abolfazil, M. K. (2015). "Why is Gold Forbidden for Men in Islam? An Original Study." Health, Spirituality and Medical Ethics 2(1), 11–14.
B. N. Mukherjee & T. N. Mukherjee (1990). *The Indian Gold*. Calcutta: Indian Museum.
Barnard, M. (2007). *The Fashion Theory*. NY: Routledge.
Barthes, R. (2009). *Mythologies*. London: Vintage Book.
Baudrillard, J. (1998). *The Consumer Society: Myth and Structure*. London: Sage Publication.
Bauman, Z. (1999). The Self in Consumer Society. *The Hedgehog Review: Critical Reflection on Contemporary Culture*, *1*(1). Retrieved October 11, 2017, from www.iasc-culture.org
Bauman, Z. (2001). Consuming Life. *Journal of Consumer Culture*. doi: 10.1177/ 146954050100100102
Bauman, Z. (2007). *Consuming Life*. UK: Polity Press.
Berger, A. A. (2014). *What Object Means: Introduction to Material Culture*. London and New York: Routledge.
Bhatt, A. (1975). *Caste, Class and Politics: An Empirical Profile of Social Stratification in Modern India*. New Delhi: Manohar Book Service.
Bhattacharya, R. (2002). *Deregulation of Gold in India: A Case Study in Deregulation of a Gold Market, Research Study Number 27*. World Gold. London: Centre for Public Policy Studies. Retrieved from www.gold.org
Bhattcharya, R. (1983). *The Imaginary and Symbolism of Gold in Literature*. PhD Department of English and Literature. University of Calcutta. Retrieved from https://shodhganga.inflibnet.ac.in/handle/10603/158333
Blackshaw, Tony. (2015). Zygmunt Bauman. London and New York: Routledge.
Bloomfield, A. I. (1959). *Monetary Policy Under the International Gold Standard: 1880–1914*. New York: Federal Reserve Bank.
Bloomfield, A. I. (1981). Gold Standard. In D. Greenwald (Ed.), *Encyclopedia of Economics* (p. 452). New York: McGraw-Hill.
Bodiciu, C. D. (2022, Aug 22). Symbiosis: A New Paradigm for Understanding How Bodies and Dress Come Together. *Fashion Theory*. doi: 10.1080/1362704X. 2022.2111020
Bohme, H. (2014). *Fetishism and Culture*. (A. Galt, Trans.) Germany: Hubert & Co. GmbH & Co.

Bose, E. (2013). "Sona na Hire Biniogay Kodor Kar?." Uttar Banga Sambadh, October 20, 9.

Bottomore, T. (2000). *A Dictionary of Marxist Thought*. New Delhi: Maya Blackwell Book.

Bourdieu, P. (1986). The Form of Capital. In J. Richardson, Handbook of Theory and Research for the Sociology of Education (pp. 241–258). Westpot: CT Greenwood.

Bourdieu, P. (1999 (1989)). *Distinction: A Social Critique of the Judgement of Taste*. (R. Nice, Trans.) London: Routledge.

Cambell, C. (1987). *The Romantic Ethic and the Spirit of Modern Consumerism*. London: Oxford, Blackwell.

Castro, J. C. L. De. (2015). The Consumer as agent in neoliberalism. Retrieved July 12, 2019 (http://www.jclcastro.com.br/downloads/Julio_Cesar_Lemes_de_Castro_-_The_consumer_as_agent_in_neoliberalism.pdf)

Chakrabarty, D. (2009). *An Archeological History: Paleolithic Beginnings to Early Historic Foundations*. India: OUP.

Dagalp, I., & Benjamin, J. H. (2022). From "aesthetic" to aestheticization: a multi-layered cultural approach. *Consumption Market & Culture*, 25, 1–20.

Daniel, D. M., & Thyumanavan, K. (2014). Impact of Organised Jewellery Retailing on Unorganized Gems and Jewellery Retailing in Madurai District With Special Reference to Madurai Gems, Jewellery and Bullion Association. *International Journal of Scientific Research*, 3(4). Retrieved from https://www.worldwidejournals.com/international-journal-of-scientific-research-(IJSR)/fileview.php?val=April_2014_1397136804_d8bdf_238.pdf

Dant, T. (2020). Consuming or Living with Thinkings? Wearing It Out. In M. Barnard (Ed.), *Fashion Theory* (pp. 504–516). London: Routledge.

Desai, A. R. (1948). *Social Background of Indian Nationalism*. Mumbai: Popular Prakash.

Desebrock, N. (2002). *An Introduction to the Indian Gold Market*. London: Virtual Metals Research & Consulting Ltd and Grendon International Research Pty Ltd.

Dhawan, S. (2019). Different Ways to Buy and Invest in Gold. Retrieved December 6, 2019, ET Online: (http://m.economicimes.com/wealth/invest/different-waysto-buy-and-invest-in-gold/articleshow/64568785.cms)

Doshi, H. C. (1998). Industrialization And Neighbourhood Communities in. Sociological Bulletin, 17(1), 19–34.

Driver, Edwin. D. (1962). Caste and Occupational Structure in Central India. *Social Force* 41(1), 26–31.

D'Souza, Errol. (2015). Gold monetization scheme for India. Economic and Political Weekly. 50 (12), 23–27.

Dube, S. C. (2004). *The Kamars*. New Delhi: OUP.

Ertimur, B., & Sandıkcı, O. (2005). Giving Gold Jewelry and Coins as Gifts: The Interplay of Utilitarianism and Symbolism.*Advances in Consumer Research*, 322–327.

Freeman, J. (1989). Rethinking Development: Modernization, Dependency, and Postmodern Politics. By David E. Apter. *American Political Science*, 83(3), 1046–1047. doi:10.2307/1962113

Freud, S. (1920). *The Three Essays on the Theory of Sextuality*. (second, Ed., & A. A. Brill, Trans.) New Tork and Washington. Retrieved 1 16, 2019, from https://www.globalgreyebooks.com/content/books/ebooks/three-essays-on-the-theory-of-sexuality.pdf

Frisby, D., & Featherstone, M. (1997). *Simmel on Culture*. London: Sage Publication.

Gerth, H. H., & Mills, C. W. (1946). *From Max Weber: Essays in Sociology.* New York: OUP.

Ghurye, G S. (1950). *Caste and Class in India.* Bombay: Popular Book Depot.

Gibbon, P., & Michael, N. (1985). Some Problems in the Political Economy of "African Socialism". In H. Bernstein, & B. K. Cambell (Eds.), *Contradictions of Accumulations in Africa: Studies in Economy and State*(p. 409). Beverly Hills: Sage Publications.

Glyn, A., & Sutcliffe, R. B. (1972). *British Capitalism, Workers and the Profits Squeeze.* Harmondsworth: Penguin Books.

Gult, H. B. (2014). *Fetishism and Culture: A Different Theory of Modernity.* Berlin: Walter De Gruyter Inc.

Hall, S. (1980). Encoding and Decoding. In S. Hall, D. Hobson, A. Love, & P. Willis (Eds.),*Culture, Media, Language: Working Papers in Cultural Studies* (p. 129). London: Hutchison.

Hancock, P. (2000). *The Body Culture and Society: An Introduction.* Buckingham: Open University Press.

Hass, J. K. (2007). *Economic Sociology.* USA: Routledge.

Huggard, E., Lonergan, P., & Overdiek, A. (2022). New Luxury Ideologies: A Shift From Building Cultural to Social Capital. *Fashion Theory,* 1–25. doi:10.1080/1362704X.2022.2117008

Imhonopi, D. d., Onifade, D. A., & Urim, U. M. (2013). Collective Behaviour and Social Movements: A Conceptual Review. *Research on Humanities and Social Sciences, 3*(10), 76–85.

India, I. (August 2016). *Guide to Excise Duty on Jewellers.* New Delhi: Taxmann.

Jha, D. N. (2004). *Early India: A Concise History.* New Delhi: Manohar Publisher.

Johnson, L. W. (1999). A Review and a Conceptual Framework of Prestige-Seeking Consumer Behavior. *Academy of Marketing Science Review, 1*(3), 1–15.

Jolly, J. (1889). The Minor Law-Books. In F. M. Mullar (Ed.), *The Sacred Book of the East.* London: Clarendon Press.

Kalidasa. (1999). *Shakuntala.* (A. W. Ryder, Trans.) Cambridge, Ontario: In Parentheses Publication, Sanskrit series.

Ketkar, S. V. (1990). *History of Caste in India.* Bangalore: Mythic Society.

Kotler, P., Keller, K. L., Koshy, A., & Jha, M. (2013). *Marketing Management A South Asian Perspective.* (14th, Ed.) Delhi: Pearson.

Krishnan, U. R. (2001). *Jewels of Nizam.* New Delhi: Department of Culture, Government of India, Shastri Bhavan.

Krishnan, U. R., & Kumar, M. S. (1999). *Indian Jewellery: Dance of the Peacock.* Bombay: Indian Book House Limited.

Laver, J. (1969). *Modesty in Dress: An Enquiry into the Fundamentals of Fashion.* London: Heinemann.

Leslie, J. (1992). *Roles and Rituals for Hindu Women.* New Delhi: Motilal Banarsidas Publisher Pvt Ltd.

Lima, M., & Fernandes, T. (2015). Relationship Bonds and Customary Loyalty: A Study Across Different Service Contexts.*International Conference on Exploring Services Science IESS* (pp. 326–339). Switzerland: Springer International Publishing. doi:10.1007/978-3-319-14980-6/26

List of Assaying & Hallmarking Centres in INDIA. (2021, 12 16). Retrieved from bis.gov.in: https://bis.gov.in/wp-content/uploads/2019/07/ERO.pdf

Litwak, E., & Szelenyi, I. (1969). Primary Group Structures and Their Functions: Kin, Neighbors, and Friends. *American Sociological Review, 34*(4), 465–481.

98   *References*

Madhukalya, A. (2021, July 12). COVID-19 impact: Indians selling off gold heirlooms to make ends meet. Retrieved from www.businesstoday.in: https://www.businesstoday.in/latest/economy/story/covid-19-impact-indians-selling-off-gold-heirlooms-to-make-ends-meet-301104-2021-07-12.

Majumdar, R. C. (2004). *The History of Bengal: Hindu Period* (vol. 1). Delhi: B. R Publication.

Majumdar, R. C., Raychaudhuri, H. C. and Datta, K. (1990). *An Advanced History of India*. London and Basingstoke: Macmillan and Company Limited.

Mehrotra, N. (2004). *Gold and Gender in India: Some Observation from South Orrisa*. Indian Anthropologist, *34*(1), 27–39.

Menon, N. (2015). *Going for Gold: Why Gold Will Always Remain the Eternal and Enduring Investment*. India: Penguin.

Metcalfe, S., Warde, A., & Harvey, M. (2003). *Market Relations and the Competitive Process: New Dynamics of Innovation & Competition*. Manchester and New York: Manchester University Press.

Mills, M. A., Class, P. J., & Diamond, S. (2003). *South Asian Folklore: An Encyclopaedia*. London: Routledge.

Milovanovic, B. (2018). Jewellery is a symbol of prestige, Power and Wealth of the Citizen of Vaminacum. (S. Golubović, & N. Mrdić, Eds.) *Vivere Militare Est – From Populus to Emperor – Loiving on the Frontier* (Monographies 68/2), *II*, 101–141.

Mitra, A. (1953). *The Tribes and Castes in West Bengal*. Retrieved from https://lsi.gov.in/MTSI_APP/(S(0ijdce45u1yrebbncootkq3c))/default.aspx: http://lsi.gov.in:8081/jspui/bitstream/123456789/5106/1/41834_1951_TRI.pdf

Morrison, K. (2006). *Marx, Durkheim, Weber: Formation of Modern Social Thought*. New Delhi: Sage Publication.

Mukherjee, R. 1958. *The Rise and Fall of the East India Company: A Sociological Appraisal*. Berlin: VED Deutscher Verlag der Wissenschaften.

Nanda, R. (1992). *The Early History of Gold in India*. New Delhi: Munshiram Manoharlal Publisher Pvt India.

Nayar, P. K. (2014). *An Introduction to Cultural Industry*. Delhi: Viva Book.

Pessemier, J. D., Palmberg, J., Kumar, M., Gopaul, K., Jia, R., Artigas, J. C., & Reade, J. (2022, September 22). Jewellery Market Structure: India Gold Market Series. Retrieved from Wold Gold Council: https://www.gold.org/goldhub/research/jewellery-market-structure-india-gold-market-series#footnote-8

PR, S. (2017). India's *Gold Market: Evolution and Innovation*. Mumbai: World Gold Council.

Raha, S. (2016). Body Image: A Reflection on Ghurye's Perspective. Social Trends, III, 119–131.

Raha, S. (2020). Body and Ornaments: A Reflection on Ghurye's Perspective. *Social Trends, VII*, 225–231.

Raha, S. (2021). The Corporate Entry into the Jewellery Market and its Socio-economic Impact on the Life of Traditional Swranakrs and Traders in Siliguri. http://hdl.handle.net/10603/403111

Raha, S. (2022). Buying belief: In India's gold jewellery market, faith and commerce are linked [Online]. *The Sociological Review Magazine*. doi:10.51428/tsr.mjli5873

Renfrew, C. (1986). Varna and the Emergence of Wealth in Prehistoric Europe. In A. Appadurai (Ed.), *The Social Life of Things: Commodities in Culture Perspective*. New York: Cambridge University Press.

Rao, I. (2017). *Cultural Governance in Indian Diamond Industry*. India: Image Publications Pvt Ltd.

Ray, M. D. (2017). Migration and Rapid Urban Growth: A study in Siliguri City. *Asian Journal of Research in Business Economics and Management*, 7(6), 117–126. doi:10.5958/2249-7307.2017.00074

Roy, S. K. (2021, March 31). Aesthetics of Living: The Deepening Crises. *Social Trends, 8*, 246–270. Retrieved from https://ir.nbu.ac.in/handle/123456789/4171

Sach, W. (1992). *The Development Dictionary*. London: Zed Books.

Sanyal, K. (2019).*Rethinking Capitalist Development: Primitive Accumulation, Governmentality & Post-Colonial Capitalism*. New Delhi: Routledge.

Schaefer, R. T. (2016). *Sociology: A Brief Introduction*. New York: McGraw Hill.

Sennettle, R. (2006). *The Culture of New Capital*. Hyderabad: Orient Longman Private Limited.

Simmel, G. (1957, May). Fashion. *The American Journal of Sociology, 62*(6), 541–558.

Simmel, G., Frisby, D., & Featherstone, M. (1997). *Simmel on Culture: Selected Writings Theory, Culture & Society*. London: Sage.

Slade, A. (2017). *Psychoanalytic: Theory and Criticism*. Hydrabad: Orient Blackswan.

Smith, H. C. (1908). *Jewellery*. New York: G. P. Putnam's Sons.

Singer, M & Cohn, B. S. (2001). *Structure and Change in Indian Society*. Jaipur and New Delhi: Rawat Publisher.

Sinha, S. (2020, August 6). Notification Loans against Gold Ornaments and Jewellery for Non-Agricultural End-uses. Retrieved from www.rbi.org.in: https://www.rbi.org.in/Scripts/NotificationUser.aspx?Id=11944&Mode=0

Stolley, K. S. (2005). *The Basics of Sociology*. London: Greenwood Press.

Swedberg, R. (1999). *Max Weber: Essays in Economic Sociology*. New Jersey: Princeton University.

Thakur, P. (2014, Dec 1). 'Mysteries Decoded: Shocking Science behind Hindu ornaments.' Retrieved from www.speakingtree.in: https://www.speakingtree.in/allslides/science-behind-hindu-ornaments

Thomas, A. (1999, Feb). What Makes Good Development Management? (Quels sont les éléments nécessaires pour une bonne gestion du développement?/O que define uma boa gestão de desenvolvimento? / ¿Qué hace a una buena gerencia del desarrollo?). *Development in Practice, 9*(1), 9–17. Retrieved June 21, 2021, from https://www.jstor.org/stable/4029703

Turner, B. (1984). *The body and Social Theory*. Thousand Oak, CA: Sage Publication.

Veblen, T. (2005). *Conspicuous Consumption*. London: Penguin Book.

Venkatesh, A. A. (2010). The Aesthetics of Luxury Fashion, Body and Identity Formation. Journal of Consumer Psychology, 20(4), 459–470. doi::10.1016/j.jcps.2010.06.011

Viswanatha, S. V. (1928). Hindu Culture in Ancient India. Delhi: Vishal Kaushik Printers.

Walter, M. (2010). *Globalisation*. London: Routledge.

Ward, R. (1990). *Governing the Market*. NJ: Princeton University Press.

Watal, S. R. (2018). *Transforming India's Gold market*. New Delhi: Government of India.

Weber, M. (1978).*Economy and Society: An Outline of Interpretive Sociology*. Berkeley, CA: University of California Press.

Weber, M. (1999). Sociological Categorial of Economic Actions. In R. Swedberg (Ed.), *Max Weber: Essays in Economic Sociology*. NJ: Princeton University Press.

Index

For Product Safety Concerns and Information please contact our EU
representative GPSR@taylorandfrancis.com
Taylor & Francis Verlag GmbH, Kaufingerstraße 24, 80331 München, Germany

* 9 7 8 1 0 3 2 7 1 7 9 4 4 *